A Larger Faith

A Larger Faith

the Book of Daniel

Glenn Parkinson

Kindle Direct Publishing

Cover design by Micki Parkinson

ISBN: 9798651702602

To the mothers, fathers, brothers and sisters
throughout my life who have modeled a larger faith.
Thanks.

Acknowledgements

One of the few benefits of the 2020 Coronavirus is more time to write. Having published a reworked sermon series through Revelation called *Tapestry*, I want to do the same for Daniel, since I view them like bookends. As always, I rely on my wife, Micki, for encouragement and art. Flo Wolfe has once again applied her English teacher's expertise to the manuscript.

This is my first project as Pastor Emeritus. Working on it during a distressing season of plague and national unrest has helped enlarge my own faith.

Contents

Preface

Ask any child, or adult for that matter, what they associate with the biblical figure of Daniel, and lions come to mind. We marvel at a faith willing to face hungry lions rather than fail in service to God. If we remember anything else from the book, it's the amazing experience of his three friends, Shadrach, Meshack and Abednego, who willingly faced a fiery furnace rather than compromise their faith. These men demonstrated a faith larger than most of us think we have, and their deliverance encourages us to believe that the Lord God is able to take care of his own.

But the Book of Daniel does more than demonstrate faith. By documenting a series of extraordinary predictive visions given to Daniel, it also describes the worldview that naturally enlarges the faith of God's people.

Here is a faith-based and rational overview of the Old Testament book which, perhaps more than any other, sets the stage for the coming of Jesus Christ and the age of gospel expansion that will conclude with his return. It is neither academic nor casual, reworked from a series of careful sermons preached in 2016. It is a natural bookend to another of my books, *"Tapestry, the Book of Revelation,"* which demonstrates that some of the key visions in

Revelation are divine amplifications of what Daniel saw earlier. Daniel and Revelation are gifts to God's people designed to help us understand and persevere during the ongoing and unavoidable tribulations of the age in which we live.

Since I will not reproduce the Book of Daniel in its entirety, the reader should keep a Bible handy and always begin by first reading the whole context flagged at the beginning of each chapter.

It is my prayer that we will see what Daniel saw and, like him, develop a larger faith to serve and glorify the Lord in our day.

Into Nebuchadnezzar's Hand

Context: Daniel 1:1-4

In the third year of the reign of Jehoiakim king of Judah, Nebuchadnezzar king of Babylon came to Jerusalem and besieged it. And the Lord gave Jehoiakim king of Judah into his hand, with some of the vessels of the house of God. And he brought them to the land of Shinar, to the house of his god, and placed the vessels in the treasury of his god. Then the king commanded Ashpenaz, his chief eunuch, to bring some of the people of Israel, both of the royal family and of the nobility, youths without blemish, of good appearance and skillful in all wisdom, endowed with knowledge, understanding learning, and competent to stand in the king's palace, and to teach them the literature and language of the Chaldeans. (Daniel 1:1-4)

Daniel was a boy of Judah, probably living in Jerusalem, during one of the most tumultuous periods in Jewish history. It was the dawn of the sixth century BC, and time was running out for the people of God.

Selected for his intelligence and good health, Daniel was almost certainly raised in a privileged Jewish home. He knew well the story of his people, how the Living God had called their ancestor Abraham to sire a nation chosen for a very special task, to be God's instrument in bringing salvation to a world lost in corruption and death. Fulfilling that role required faith in the Living God as their Lord and Savior. God had miraculously delivered Abraham's children from bitter bondage in Egypt and given them a land where they could become a light to all non-Jews (Gentiles) as they pursued the moral and social excellence he commanded.

But from the founding of this unique nation, Moses made it quite clear that persistent faithlessness and disobedience would bring painful chastisement. The Lord could not extend his salvation to all the world through a people who took his name in vain and lived lives as empty as those in the nations surrounding them. For generations, God's prophets warned of the dire consequences of religious hypocrisy and unrepentant corruption. Already, foolish civil war had divided the nation. The ten northern tribes of Israel had been conquered by Assyria and scattered forever. Only Judah in the south remained to worship at the Jerusalem Temple and carry on God's great mission.

Two boyhood heroes

Faithfulness had been waning in Judah for some time, as well, but at the end of the seventh century BC a revival brought hope. King Josiah called Judah back to faith in the Living God.

> And the king stood by the pillar and made a covenant before the Lord, to walk after the Lord and to keep his commandments and his testimonies and his statutes with all his heart and all his soul, to perform the words of this covenant that were written in this book. And all the people joined in the covenant. (2 Kings 23:3)

Josiah's reforms were extensive. He tore down a multitude of idolatrous shrines. He put an end to barbarous human sacrifice. He had the Law of Moses read publicly, celebrated the Passover for the first time in generations and restored a faithful priesthood. Judging from his later life, Daniel's boyhood had been shaped by two great men, and in his early years, Josiah surely had been one of them. Josiah's example introduced Daniel to a great and good God worthy of worship who was determined to bring the light of salvation to all the world. "Before him there was no king like him, who turned to the Lord with all his heart and with all his soul and with all his might, according to all the Law of Moses, nor did any like him arise after him" (2 Kings 23:25).

One can only imagine the shock and dismay when, after over thirty years of glorious rule, Josiah was killed in battle against an advancing Egyptian army. That's when everything began to unravel. Josiah's sons did not exercise the faith of their father. In the terse language of the Old Testament, they "did what was evil in the sight of the Lord." In Daniel's teen years, he saw Josiah's emphasis on true faith and moral integrity fade away. In its place arose intense political maneuvering that sided with either Egypt or Babylon in an attempt to win favor with whoever seemed most likely to became the dominant superpower. In that effort, the new kings were supported by the entire religious establishment. Priest and prophet pretended to continue Josiah's faith, but their religion lapsed into hypocrisy and superstition. They preached that God would bless them simply because of their original calling and the existence of the Lord's Temple in their midst. The moral integrity that arises from true worship evaporated.

Of all the religious leaders, only a handful remained faithful to the Lord. The clearest voice among them was the second major influence in Daniel's young life, the prophet Jeremiah. Jeremiah reached for the faith which had fallen with Josiah. He lifted up the Lord as alone worthy of our worship and obedience, and repeated the warning of Moses and Isaiah that turning away from faith in the Lord would bring terrible consequences. While other religious leaders mindlessly chanted "the Temple of the Lord" as their hope of salvation, Jeremiah expressed the Lord's displeasure at the general shallowness and hypocrisy. "Judah did not return to me with her whole heart, but in pretense, declares the Lord" (Jeremiah 3:10).

Jeremiah declared that God's patience was at an end. As a result, the might of Babylon would soon be loosed upon the nation of Judah, bringing Abraham's children into bondage once again. No one wanted to listen to this message. Jeremiah exposed corrupt prophets, and in return they skewered him in their sermons. He challenged the paltry faith of the priests, and the chief priest had him flogged. He called upon the king to repent, trusting in God instead of his political schemes, and the king had him thrown into a pit.

Taming an empire

Just four years after King Josiah's death, King Nebuchadnezzar of Babylon successfully subdued the land of Israel in his effort to secure border territory that would contain his rival, Egypt. The inflammatory politics of Josiah's sons would bring the Babylonian king back a few years later in a second invasion, this time to smash Jerusalem and utterly destroy the holy Temple.

Although the Lord's prophets warned and predicted this would happen, for Nebuchadnezzar, it was just part of his frontier strategy. Having subdued Judah, the next question was how to keep it loyal. Given that local leaders had rebelled against his rule once, what could he do to insure their subjection? There are several schools of thought about how an empire can best secure the long-term subjugation of a conquered people. Some are humiliated by those who conquer them, stripped of dignity and the power to rebel (think of Germany after the First World War, or the Indian nations in frontier America). Others have the opposite experience, offered a new and better future by their conquerors (think of Germany again, but this time under the Marshall Plan after World War II).

Nebuchadnezzar pursued both strategies with a single tactic. He claimed the best and brightest youth of Judah, thus robbing their future leadership while supplying Babylon's insatiable need for talent. His goal was to turn these young people into Babylonian leaders and professionals who could attain greater stature under him than they would in their "backward" homeland. They would prove useful whether they served well in his court, or were sent back as loyal subjects to govern their ancestral people.

Daniel was among the Jews taken after the first invasion. Many more followed.

What Daniel lost

To understand the "larger faith" Daniel will display over his life, it's important to appreciate the loss this teenager faced on the long journey from Jerusalem to Babylon. He wasn't going to come home after college or visit over the holidays. Daniel would never see his family again. He would never again see Jerusalem or Judah, the house of his youth or the streets where he grew up. He would never again see the Temple, hear its singing, see its sacrifices or celebrate any of the great feasts. He would be expected to learn and speak the Babylonian language for the rest of his life, as well as eat Babylonian food, wear Babylonian clothes, celebrate Babylonian holidays, use Babylonian money and appreciate Babylonian music and art.

Perhaps hardest of all for a young man, he probably faced the violation of his sexuality and hopes of marriage and a family. The former Jewish King Hezekiah had received the prophetic word, "And some of your descendants, your own flesh and blood that will be born to you, will be taken away, and they will become eunuchs in the palace of the king of Babylon" (2 Kings 20:18). Indeed, in surrounding cultures the castration of slaves was common. Daniel had become a slave. There is no record that he had a family. And Daniel was assigned to be trained by Ashpenaz, the king's "chief eunuch."

For Daniel, slavery would provide a magnificent education for a useful career. If he applied himself, he would be treated well. But that privilege would come at a horrific cost. It would cost him everything he knew and everything he hoped for physically and emotionally. And it was Nebuchadnezzar's aim to take his spiritual identity, as well. Erase his faith in the Living God of Abraham, in revelation, in the covenant of salvation, and overwrite it with cultural deities that cultivated the worship of Babylon itself. This was the end of Daniel's world.

Such catastrophic loss would bring most people to a fork in their spiritual path. The obvious logical conclusion would be that God had abandoned his people. If so, either his promises were no good, or his power useless against the gods of Babylon, or perhaps Israel's God did not really exist. There would be no cultural benefit in continuing to worship the Lord. Best to leave it all behind and put together the best life possible, with new gods in a new reality.

Except for one thing. Something so unique and important that Daniel stressed it in the very first sentences of his written work: "In the third year of the reign of Jehoiakim king of Judah, Nebuchadnezzar king of Babylon came to Jerusalem and besieged it. *And the Lord gave Jehoiakim king of Judah into his hand*" (Daniel 1:1-2, emphasis added).

The Lord *gave* Judah into Nebuchadnezzar's hand. Daniel was not on his way to Babylon because Israel lost a battle. It was not because Nebuchadnezzar won that Daniel had personally lost everything he held dear. It was because the Lord *gave* Judah, gave Jerusalem, and therefore gave *him*, into Babylonian captivity. By warning of it beforehand, Jeremiah (and Isaiah and even Moses long before) demonstrated that this did not happen because the Lord was defeated by Babylonian gods. Rather, the calamity was God's purposeful response to Israel's sin. This insight had so many implications.

The sovereignty of the Lord God has no bounds

Israel believed that all other gods are manmade. Only the Creator is real, and he revealed himself to Israel with the personal name, *Yahweh*, which means "I Am Who I Am," but is traditionally written as "the Lord." Israel saw the power of the Lord in their initial exodus and many times thereafter as he won battles, stopped plagues, eased famines and the like. Daniel had personally seen the Lord's goodness and power in Josiah's career.

But now, Daniel saw the Lord's power in another way. Mighty Babylon was unwittingly fulfilling the word of the Lord's prophet, Jeremiah. The Lord chose Israel for his people, but his control has no boundaries. Surely, when Solomon said, "The king's heart is a stream of water in the hand of the Lord; he turns it wherever he will" (Proverbs 21:1), that is true of all kings whether they know it or not, including Nebuchadnezzar.

God's plan would be advanced through the exile

The Lord had called Israel for a purpose:

> Now the Lord said to Abram, "Go from your country and your kindred and your father's house to the land that I will show you. And I will make of you a great nation, and I will bless you and make your name great, so that you will be a blessing. I will bless those who bless you, and him who dishonors you I will curse, and in you all the families of the earth shall be blessed." (Genesis 12:1-3)

Abraham had done nothing to earn this promise; it was all of grace. It was a promise that used the earthly inheritance of "a great nation" to communicate an eternal blessing offered to the whole world (Hebrews 11:8-16). This promise was nothing less than what was later called the *gospel* (Galatians 3:3-9).

When Jesus came to fulfill this promise, he made it clear that the nations would believe that God's offer of grace is real when his people are "the light of the world," passionate about following him in their lifestyle

(Matthew 5:1-16; John 15:1-8; 17:20-23). This had always been true, going back to Israel's calling to be a light to the Gentiles (Isaiah 49:6; 60:3; Luke 2:32; Acts 13:47).

Israel took this calling for granted when, as a people, they manifested no interest in God's character. Josiah had been Israel's last hope of reform. After much patient long-suffering, God proceeded to chasten his people in order to underscore the true character of his kingdom. Happily, this action would also set the stage for another public demonstration of grace on the world stage, as he forgave a repentant people and brought them back to their land.

Choosing a larger faith

Confident in the goodness of the Lord's character that he had seen modeled in Josiah, and in the universal sovereignty demonstrated by the predictions of Jeremiah and the prophets before him, Daniel surrendered the life he had anticipated, for whatever God would give him. We know this because of his first actions in Babylon (the focus of the next chapter). "Surrendering" may sound euphemistic, since there wasn't anything he could have done about his situation, anyway. But Daniel's surrender was proved genuine by his devotion and obedience to God. Patient endurance illustrates more faith than any aggressive or stubborn response ever could.

When I think of such surrender, I think of a visit from Richard and Sabina Wurmbrand to my church back in the 1980's. Richard was a Christian pastor who, in the 1950's and 60's was imprisoned in Communist Rumania for fourteen years because he would not support communism. The abuse he suffered led to permanent injuries. His wife also spent three years in a labor camp. I remember them as two of the sweetest people I've ever met. They spoke to us of God's love and forgiveness, illustrating their message with a forgiving encounter they once had with a former prison guard. During discussion afterwards, someone asked Richard how he could live with that regime taking away fourteen years of his life? I'll never forget his quiet reply, "They didn't take those years. I gave them."

Because of what Daniel did when he arrived in Babylon, I have to think that he also decided to give everything Babylon had taken—in essence, give or dedicate his life to God's glory. In all that follows, there will not be one word of complaint or self-pity. Daniel will even shoulder some of the blame for Israel's sin.

What inspired and sustained such faith? Richard and Sabina had the example of Christ. What did Daniel have?

I believe that while Daniel may have come to *love* the Lord through Josiah, he believed God was *real* because Jeremiah opened Daniel's eyes to the Living God who alone shapes history—not just Israel's history, but the history of the world. Daniel began with at least a germ of this insight, and God responded with exceptional visions which, in turn, continued to enlarge his faith.

An enslaved teenager on his way to an uncertain future faced a choice: Affirm a pragmatic religion shaped by Babylon. Or whole-heartedly embrace a larger faith in the real, sovereign God who shapes history to redeem mankind. As Daniel's story unfolds, it does not take long to see what he chose, and how the Lord responded by making Daniel one of his greatest servants of all time.

The King's Food

Context: Daniel 1:5-21

The king assigned them a daily portion of the food that the king ate, and of the wine that he drank. They were to be educated for three years, and at the end of that time they were to stand before the king. Among these were Daniel, Hananiah, Mishael, and Azariah of the tribe of Judah. And the chief of the eunuchs gave them names: Daniel he called Belteshazzar, Hananiah he called Shadrach, Mishael he called Meshach, and Azariah he called Abednego.
But Daniel resolved that he would not defile himself with the king's food, or with the wine that he drank. (Daniel 1:5-8)

Daniel arrived in Babylon in the company of three fellow Jewish slaves. If Daniel, Hananiah, Mishael and Azariah had not known each other previously, then they must have become fast friends on the long journey to their new world. It becomes pretty clear that they shared the same faith and stuck together as much as possible through the three years of their initial training. Daniel clearly kept up with their careers thereafter.

The first thing that their overseer/trainer Ashpenaz did was to give them shiny new Babylonian names. Daniel became Belteshazzar (though he is still called

Daniel most often in his own writings), and his three friends received names that are still well known today: Shadrach, Meshach and Abednego.

It is fascinating and instructive to observe how Daniel and his friends successfully navigated a foreign culture in a way that maintained their larger faith. They would need to establish thoughtful boundaries. But what boundaries? What could they accept of Babylonian culture, and what could they not? In what areas would they relent and in what areas take a stand?

For example, there are many firm Bible believers today who would staunchly object to accepting the names of pagan gods, or idols. "Belteshazzar" referred to Bel or Marduk, the chief Babylonian deity, "Shadrach" and "Meshack" referred to Aku, the Moon god, and "Abednego" meant servant of Nebu, patron god of scribes. But they accepted these names (distasteful to them, no doubt) without objection. Apparently, it was not an important enough issue to contest—not a hill to die on.

But immediately after the change of their names arose a faith-issue so important that they did, respectfully, oppose the King and risk their future.

Remembering who I am

"The king assigned them a daily portion of the food that the king ate, and of the wine that he drank." But Daniel "resolved that he would not defile himself" with the king's food and wine (Daniel 1:5,8). He asked his overseer to please feed them simple meals of vegetables and water. Not believing that these young men would appear as healthy with that menu as they would with rich food and wine, Ashpenaz was hesitant. So, Daniel proposed a test. Let them eat a simple menu for ten days, and then see if they appeared any worse off. Their trainer agreed. When they actually seemed healthier than the others after ten days, Ashpenaz continued them on that regimen without the king being any the wiser.

But why was Daniel concerned that this food would "defile" him? One common explanation is that the Babylonian menu violated Old Testament food laws. Daniel gave no further explanation, so this may be what Ashpenaz assumed.

Or was it what Daniel *wanted* him to assume? In fact, we don't know that any of his meals would have actually violated Old Testament food laws. Certainly most of them would not. If ceremonial defilement was the reason, why not object only to specific menu items? More importantly, there is no Old Testament prohibition against wine. If ceremonial defilement was the reason, why object to wine?

If Jewish dietary laws were not Daniel's concern, then could Daniel have been concerned about his health? Daniel and his friends did look healthier after vegetarian meals. But dietary preference would not have been a sufficient reason to circumvent the king's order. More importantly, "defilement" suggested an ethical concern of some sort.

Some call Daniel's chosen diet a "partial fast" for spiritual purity, but there is nothing suggesting that this was only a temporary self-denial. The arrangement lasted at least for the three years Daniel trained under Ashpenaz. Also, Daniel would later fast for specific purposes (e.g., Daniel 9:3), and there is nothing there to suggest that his idea of fasting was to abstain only from rich food.

Perhaps it was the source of the food. It is likely that all the meat was first offered to idols. We see such hesitance to eat meat offered to idols later in the New Testament. But the Apostle Paul would explain that there is no real defilement from eating such food (because, he would say, idolatrous gods do not actually exist), though he did respect a believer's reluctance to do so. At any rate, this could not have been Daniel's objection, because the vegetables he ate would have been offered to Babylonian gods, as well.

It may not be possible to know the exact nature of Daniel's concern, but the most likely reason may relate to this period of initial Babylonian indoctrination. King Nebuchadnezzar shared with them "food that the king ate," that is, the very best food available, taken from his own larder. Sumptuous dining was one of the perks designed to turn their hearts away from their original allegiance and cement their loyalty to the king. It was like access to a royal limousine, or to areas and events open only to VIPs.

Perks like these are designed to create an "understanding." Those who receive extra privileges are expected to be extra loyal. In other words, to eat the king's food meant that you are willing to be the king's man. Share what the king owns, and it is understood that the king owns you. Eating the king's food meant that he could not only ask you to do your job, he could ask a great deal more. In fact, he could ask anything, and you had already made the choice to do it. Nebuchadnezzar wanted loyal retainers, not reluctant slaves. He had smashed Jerusalem and its Temple, and deported the best and brightest. Now it was time to offer juicy rewards for compliance.

Daniel's faith had already endured Nebuchadnezzar's intimidating stick; now he was determined not to be seduced by the king's carrots. Daniel's secret decision to not eat from the king's table was his way of affirming his spiritual identity and allegiance. He had nothing against the food itself, and he had every intention of serving the king well. But he was determined to be the Lord's man, not the king's.

For Daniel, this meant jealously guarding his spiritual perspective. Simply put, Daniel needed to remember that God is more sovereign and more glorious than the Babylonian king. God is more powerful and more worthy than the king, and Daniel needed to call that to mind every day. He believed the predictive prophecies that had declared how God would incorporate an exile into his plan to rebuild a strong relationship with his people. The exile was God's idea before it was Nebuchadnezzar's. Babylon was truly mighty, but it had been made mighty by God in order to accomplish God's plans.

Daniel chose to believe these things deeply, even though he had become a slave of Babylon. Perhaps it was even because he was a slave that he felt the need to hang his life on the sovereign grace of Israel's God. Hadn't the Lord God called Abraham to father a nation when nearly 100 years old? Hadn't he found Israel in Egyptian bondage and delivered them with a mighty hand and an outstretched arm? The Lord God is able to raise up and bring low … and raise up again. The more the king's training tried to impress Babylon's glory onto Daniel's soul, the more important it was for Daniel to affirm that God is far more glorious. After all, who is more sovereign: the one who accomplishes great deeds, or the one who decrees those deeds and gives the strength necessary to accomplish them?

The more Nebuchadnezzar flaunted his ability to bless, the tighter Daniel held on to his conviction that the best blessing follows after God's glory. If the Living God had brought Israel low using Nebuchadnezzar's unwitting cooperation, then the same Living God would lift Israel up again, and lift up his servant Daniel as well.

But keeping one's heart fixed on God's preeminence is not easy when constantly seduced by special privilege. Daniel could not stop the Babylonian army from abducting him, but he might be able to do something about the constant drip of the king's alluring perks. The students of the royal court shared the same luxurious larder as the king, but they did not actually eat in the king's presence. Point being that Nebuchadnezzar only knew what their overseer, Ashpenaz, told him about what they ate. So all Daniel had to do was make a private arrangement with Ashpenaz.

Daniel's overseer didn't really care why Daniel and his friends wanted vegetables, as long as the young men performed well and looked healthy (his livelihood and welfare depended on that). Daniel reasonably suggested a test to see if a simple diet would do any harm. It did not, so Daniel and his friends were given the freedom to set their own diet. And if Ashpenaz was able to find some other use for all that superb food and drink, so much the better. In the end, the king would never know.

Daniel and his three friends avoided the succulent seduction of the king's food throughout their three years of education. They recognized the danger of becoming "yes men" to the king, losing sight of the greater glory of God by being bought off with luxurious dishes and fine wine. Their strategy was brilliantly simple: make each and every meal a private affirmation of their primary allegiance.

Every day of their training, these four young men were indoctrinated into Babylonian culture, language, religion, politics and manners. Every day, the glory of Babylon was paraded before them in preparation for the privilege of serving the greatest king on earth.

And every day they would have a main meal, like all the other students. But these four would eat together because they shared the same dietary arrangement. Their agreement with Ashpenaz assured that they would have daily fellowship with the only others who longed for a larger faith. And while those around them became accustomed to the beneficence of King Nebuchadnezzar, they took their daily bread with the God who is a greater King than any man and who provides even kings with food. They remembered the prophecies of Israel's exile, and what they proved concerning who is truly sovereign. The cost of this daily fellowship to honor the Living God was to have nothing more exciting than water and vegetables. But the plan worked brilliantly, enabling them to shield and nourish each other's faith through the long process of indoctrination.

Guarding their heart by glorifying God above all paid immediate dividends. They became men whom God was prepared to bless. At their final exam,

> … in every matter of wisdom and understanding about which the king inquired of them, he found them ten times better than all the magicians and enchanters that were in all his kingdom. (Daniel 1:20)

While Daniel stayed in the king's court, as the years went by it seems that his three friends were scattered throughout the empire. After they finished their education and were given positions with their own retainers, it is likely that they allowed themselves more than vegetables. But their indomitable focus on glorifying God had already been forged during those challenging early years of preparation.

Who am I?

Each day, our surrounding culture offers us perks that create an "understanding." A person's soul can be bought in just about any environment: business, government, family, virtually any human institution, actually. We might have what it takes to resist an open bribe to do something that grossly violates our conscience. But resistance becomes increasingly difficult over time as we come to depend on a lifestyle which disobedience would jeopardize. At that point, luxuries become the gilded cage of slaves.

A larger faith expects to find our personal good while in pursuit of God's glory. When we are conditioned to see what's good for us in terms of perks provided by the world, faith shrinks. God's plan for human history and eternity becomes less important, more abstract and less relevant. The more we become dependent on daily creature comforts and special privileges, the less we can afford any faithfulness to God which might forfeit what we are accustomed to.

The problem is, the world's perks keep coming at us. And it is expected that we take them, along with the attached entanglements. Perhaps we can take a cue from Daniel as to what to do.

Daniel demonstrates that the most important battle is always the one for our soul, our allegiance. The battle is not associated with any one particular cultural demand. God expects us to honor many aspects of our culture, as long as we always put him first. There are few hard and fast rules to this. Our best preparation is to kindle our allegiance afresh every day. It is a losing strategy to allow a seduction to have unopposed access to our soul, and then try to play catch-up in the face of temptation. Daniel shows us the value of an explicit, daily exercise of faith.

As a young Christian, I was regularly lectured about the importance of a "Quiet Time" of Bible study and prayer as the key to sustaining a strong faith. Unfortunately, I just didn't get the point. I thought the few minutes thrown at prayer and Bible study were next to useless—there were better ways to pray and to study. It was not until years later that I finally understood what I imagine everyone else knew: quiet times are about communion with God, reflecting on who he is, who I am, and who we are together. Bible study and prayer are simply tools for communion—not the end, but the means.

This student pact of Daniel and his friends also shows us the value of fellowship. We can't maintain a consistent practice of faith on our own. We need each other. As Solomon said,

> Two are better than one, because they have a good reward for their toil. For if they fall, one will lift up his fellow. But woe to him who is alone when he falls and has not another to lift him up! (Ecclesiastes 4:9-10)

This goes double for matters of faith. Would Daniel have developed into the man he became had he pondered his recurring plate of vegetables all by himself? Doubt and self pity are far more dangerous when we walk alone. As long as even one fellow traveler has the faith I need when I am distracted or discouraged, he or she can lift me up. Later, I can do the lifting for them. It is a powerful strategy.

We also see in this chapter of Daniel's story the value of establishing spiritual commitments early in life, or early in a new phase of life. Proverbs urges, "Keep your heart with all vigilance, for from it flow the springs of life" (Proverbs 4:23). Nothing is more important than explicitly cultivating the convictions we are prepared to live by. We need to know what we know about God and ourselves, the reason he made us and what we are doing about it. The swirl and action of daily life obscure our deepest beliefs the way the action of a baseball game covers home plate with dirt. We must constantly brush the dust and grit off of what we believe, so it can remain the touchstone and focal point of our endeavors.

In addition, there is something to be said for keeping our deepest communion with God private. At the time, no one knew the eating arrangement of those four young men except Ashpenaz, and even he did not understand where they were going with it. The power of faith is generated deep in one's soul, where others cannot see. "Do not let your left hand know what your right hand is doing," said Jesus (Matthew 6:3).

Certainly Daniel knew the stories of King David. When Saul was surprised that young David was willing to go up against Goliath. David responded,

"Your servant used to keep sheep for his father. And when there came a lion, or a bear, and took a lamb from the flock, I went after him and struck him and delivered it out of his mouth. And if he arose against me, I caught him by his beard and struck him and killed him. Your servant has struck down both lions and bears, and this uncircumcised Philistine shall be like one of them, for he has defied the armies of the living God.

And David said, "The Lord who delivered me from the paw of the lion and from the paw of the bear will deliver me from the hand of this Philistine." (1 Samuel 17:34-37)

When tending the flock by himself, David could have easily explained away the loss of a sheep to a lion. Instead, he was willing to risk his life out of simple faith that the Lord would help him honor his father and his God. The character and faith which David developed in private, when no one could see, was later available when God's honor involved something the whole world—and all of history—would see.

Wanting a larger faith

Daniel's experience with lions would not come until much later. But like David, he cultivated his inner character in private. Daniel and his friends established the Lord as the center focus of their heart. They created a daily reminder of God's preeminence in their lives, a small and private sacrifice which only they and the Lord understood.

Such things carry immense weight with God. We see that in the New Testament story of the widow who came to the Temple to offer her meager daily food allotment as a gift. She did her best to go unnoticed because it was a private gift to God. Little did she realize who it was who had just taken a break from teaching to rest against the wall where Temple offerings were deposited, sitting so close that he could see what she quietly dropped in as an offering. Jesus was deeply moved by her private devotion, so much so that when she was out of earshot, he called together his disciples to point her out as a model of faith.

With the same interest and joy, the Living God saw Daniel, Shadrach, Meshack and Abednego gather around an arranged meal of vegetables and water. He saw them privately rehearse their faith in him in an effort to insulate themselves from faith-leeching favors. He watched them do that over a thousand times.

These young men were serious about faith. They wanted a larger faith. A faith much bigger than their personal experience and short human lifespan. A faith centered on God's promise to redeem all nations through a salvation manifested in Israel, something that had already consumed centuries and might require more centuries before the promised blessings came in fullness. The Books of Moses laid the groundwork for God's future plan. The Psalms celebrated it and the Prophets outlined it theologically. But these young men nurtured a larger faith without any clear or specific idea of how God's plans were slated to work out.

After a thousand meals of vegetables and water, the Lord God would change that. The Lord would reveal to Daniel a plan woven into real-world empires, cultural movements and history-shaping events centuries in their future. He would place the development of his kingdom, the Kingdom of God, in the context of identifiable human empires. He would trace the future of Israel in his plan to bless all nations. He would specify with uncanny accuracy the exact point in time when this plan would swing from promise to fulfillment. He would reveal one of the seminal titles that his Christ would use to describe himself. He would characterize what would be called "the last days" as a sweeping epoch of spiritual growth and spiritual conflict, and he would describe it so vividly to Daniel that it would form the visual vocabulary for the climactic closing book of the New Testament.

Faith often starts out small, perhaps being taken to church as a child or making a scripted profession after an evangelistic presentation. A larger faith, however, requires a conscious centering of one's soul in the Living God whose agenda spans all of human history. It is a conscious decision which, like concrete, takes a while to fully set. But when it does, it becomes a foundation God can use to build his kingdom.

A God Who Reveals Mysteries

Context: Daniel 2:1-30

> In the second year of the reign of Nebuchadnezzar, Nebuchadnezzar had dreams; his spirit was troubled, and his sleep left him. Then the king commanded that the magicians, the enchanters, the sorcerers, and the Chaldeans be summoned to tell the king his dreams. So they came in and stood before the king. And the king said to them, "I had a dream, and my spirit is troubled to know the dream." Then the Chaldeans said to the king in Aramaic, "O king, live forever! Tell your servants the dream, and we will show the interpretation." The king answered and said to the Chaldeans, "The word from me is firm: if you do not make known to me the dream and its interpretation, you shall be torn limb from limb, and your houses shall be laid in ruins. But if you show the dream and its interpretation, you shall receive from me gifts and rewards and great honor. Therefore show me the dream and its interpretation." (Daniel 2:1-6)

The king had a nightmare. Most people have nightmares occasionally. Maybe you're being chased, or falling, or unprepared for some kind of meeting. The terror of most nightmares is balanced by the exquisite joy of waking up to discover that you were only dreaming, and the nightmare does not reflect reality.

King Nebuchadnezzar was one of the most powerful and fearless kings of all time. He had faced opposing armies and ruled an empire. He had probably even chaired committee meetings. All to say that there was not much that could scare him.

But this nightmare shook him hard. It was so vivid that he could remember every detail. It was so bizarre and threatening that he couldn't let it go. He had dreamed of a huge, strangely-constructed statue, probably with his face, and saw it violently demolished by a boulder—a boulder that then grew into a mountain. Was this an omen? An omen of what? The scope of the disaster suggested more than his demise ... the wholesale destruction of his kingdom? his legacy?

Wise Men

Nebuchadnezzar followed his first instinct, which was to call for his Magi to interpret the dream. Magi were the priest-scholars of Babylon. They were consulted about politics, natural science, culture and religion. Zoroaster had a large influence on the group's development. He believed in one god, and believed that through study we could find connections between god and our world.

Babylonians were among the first to carefully study the universe in an attempt to extract meaning for our lives. They searched for the essential building blocks of matter and energy in a discipline called alchemy. As their four elements of earth, air, fire and water expanded, alchemy later became what we call chemistry. They systematically searched for meaningful patterns connecting the stars, planets and seasons in what was known as astrology. Those meticulous observations developed into what we call astronomy. They were the first to fluently speak of the language of science, which is mathematics. They created the most important number of all: zero, a place-holder enabling advanced computation. They created the numerical system based on 60 which we still use today to measure both time and angles. They got very close to square roots and quadratic equations, and even seemed to understand the gist of Pythagoras' theorem before the Greeks invented theorems.

The Magi, or Wise Men, of the sixth century BC were not fools or charlatans. They tried to observe and deduce how the forces of the universe work to impact us. Today, we call the study of universal forces physics. Since they tied their study to religion as well, we call their earlier version metaphysics. We may be tempted to smile at their notion that everything is made of earth, air, fire and water, but if you had no exposure to modern chemistry, how would you describe the world you see? The point is that they were among the first, if not the first, to try to describe reality systematically, try to find order and meaning in the universe we experience.

As such, they were held in high regard, the keepers of theories, mathematical calculations and divine wisdom which the uneducated could not grasp. When the king called for an emergency meeting of the Magi, it was like summoning the best from NASA, MIT and CERN. In that society, they believed that dreams could be connected to real events, and what Nebuchadnezzar saw would have seemed to him like a killer asteroid targeting a bullseye with his face on it.

But never wise enough

What makes this story so poignant is the other side of the king's fear. Yes, he feared the dream. But he also feared that the brightest and the best really didn't know as much as everyone thought they did. When you're talking about a drought or an investment decision, you can be fluid in your planning. But the obliteration of the empire? The possible destruction of an entire legacy? Nebuchadnezzar could not afford a guess. He did not want probabilities. He certainly didn't want to be at the mercy of academics who were afraid to look bad. They needed to *know* truth, and he needed to know that they knew it.

It may be that any thinking person has at one time or another questioned authorities he or she had previously accepted. Thinking people realize that the best authorities can be mistaken. Aristotle famously asserted, and many believed, that men have more teeth than women (he must not have even checked, for it is not true). As long as life is pleasant or bearable, there is no reason to question what you believe. But when fear stalks your soul, the need for certainty becomes desperate. Nebuchadnezzar feared the dream, but he also feared that those he depended on for knowledge might not really know what they were doing.

So the assembled men of wisdom received a shocking demand. They must explain to the king his dream. And to prove that it was the correct explanation, they had to first tell him what the dream was! That's right, he did not relate to them a dream and ask them to interpret it. Rather, he demanded that they first describe his dream, and then explain it. And to make things interesting, he promised them a very unpleasant death if they failed, and immense honor and wealth if they succeeded.

At that point, the king was not the only one afraid. These scientist-priests would not be able to live up to their reputation.

It is still true today that society likes to turn its scientists into priests—that is, invest in them authority to not only describe the universe, but explain its purpose and meaning. But modern scientists are no more competent to make this connection than their Babylonian counterparts. Science is about making mathematical models to describe what we observe. Science constantly changes, constantly improves as more data is available. We can describe the universe so much better now than we could even 100 years ago, let alone two and half millennia in the past. That is, we can account for much more data in our models.

This is not to say that we have figured out how everything works. Not yet. Today, astrophysicists postulate that 27% of all matter in the universe is *dark matter*, and that 68% of all energy in the universe is *dark energy*. Ask an astrophysicist what those things are, and he or she will tell you that they are simply labels for something we don't understand at all. In other words, today's science can describe only 5% of the matter and energy in the universe! This is not a problem with science; it's the business of science to keep collecting more data in order to fabricate a more comprehensive understanding.

But even after dark matter and energy are one day fully accounted for, science will still be no closer to addressing Nebuchadnezzar's essential question, "What does it all mean?" Science excels in the "what," but is clueless as to the "why." By "why," I don't mean how cause and effect works on a physical level, but rather the meaning of the causes, the *purpose* behind the way things are, and most personally, the purpose of *me*.

Since the Enlightenment, there has been a growing despair that, since science cannot answer purpose-questions, then such questions cannot be answered, or alternately, that no human purpose exists. I've lost count of the scientists who try to cheer us up by pointing out that we are "star dust," that we are made of the stuff of stars. But how can you get meaning out of random dust? You can't. We find, as Nebuchadnezzar did, that meaning is not found in science. And that's not the fault of science; the fault is in expecting scientists to also be priests.

The God who is really there

Back to our story, Daniel realizes that the Magi will fail, and when they do, not only they, but also the students in training (like him) will also be put to death. So he calls his friends and they pray for God's deliverance. God answers their prayers, and gives Daniel a vision of the king's dream, along with an understanding of its meaning.

When Daniel is granted an audience with the king, Nebuchadnezzar asks if Daniel can do what the established Magi cannot. Daniel replied that, honestly, he cannot. What he said was,

> No wise men, enchanters, magicians, or astrologers can show to the king the mystery that the king has asked, but there is a God in heaven who reveals mysteries, and he has made known to King Nebuchadnezzar what will be in the latter days. (Daniel 2:27-28)

We will study the dream and its meaning in the next chapter. The point here is that Daniel could not do any better than the current Wise Men. Even having spiritual sensitivities, or having a strong faith in something or other, doesn't really help. Faith may recognize meaning when it sees it or generate a false sense of meaning, but our sensation of faith cannot *create* real purpose. Real purpose involves intention, and we did not intentionally create ourselves. We define the purpose of things that we create or do, but we cannot define our own essential purpose as human beings. Our purpose can only be defined by our Creator. The Wise Men demonstrated wisdom when they told the king, "There is not a man on earth who can meet the king's demand .... no one can show it to the king except the gods, whose dwelling is not with flesh" (Daniel 2:10-11).

Daniel agreed with them entirely. Questions of meaning and purpose, the *why* questions, cannot be answered by science and its observation of what, how, and when. "Why?" is a question only God can answer, and God does not dwell with us. To put it another way, God and mankind are not on speaking terms. This was the first thing Daniel would have learned from his nation's Bible, the Book of Genesis specifically. Humanity made a terrible choice at the beginning of civilization to suppress the conscience that God built into us, in favor of pretending whatever we feel like is right (Romans 2:15-16, in context). Rejecting the conscience God gave us has effectively sabotaged our relationship with him, and made God invisible. Insisting to define ourselves, we have lost all sure knowledge of our purpose. And the only way we can discover it is for God to speak, to reveal it to us if he so wishes, and for us to believe him.

"There is a God in heaven who reveals mysteries." The very essence of the faith Daniel had worked so very hard to maintain is that the Living God reveals himself. That is the meaning of the name he related to Abraham and Moses, "I Am Who I Am." God is not who we define him to be. The eternal God alone defines himself. And if the uncreated God defines himself, then he surely defines his creations—in particular, who we are and why we're here. That is true for all humanity. It was true for Nebuchadnezzar and his legacy.

Daniel's response to the king tells us a great deal about his faith. Daniel did not believe that his faith made him better than other people. It wasn't about Daniel winning or coming out on top. "No wise men ... can show to the king the mystery that the king has asked." There is no special inherent worth attached to Daniel or Daniel's people, the Jews. The Jews were indeed chosen by God, but chosen in spite of their shortcomings, to function as a vessel for God's revelation to all nations.

Daniel could describe Nebuchadnezzar's dream, not because Daniel could figure it out, but because God told him. And the fact that God had told Daniel the king's dream convinced Nebuchadnezzar that Daniel could also hear from God how to interpret it.

A faith based on revelation

When young Daniel told Nebuchadnezzar exactly what he had dreamed, the king fulfilled his promise to shower Daniel with wealth and power. Despite his youth, Daniel attained an influence in the Babylonian court above all other Magi. He actually became the leader of the Wise Men. His special standing would endure even the political shift from Babylonian to Mede/Persian rule years later. He became the one truly indispensable man in the kingdom, because he knew the God who reveals mysteries and the course of empires.

How would the other Magi have reacted to Daniel? Later, we will discover that he had powerful enemies. It must be difficult to be upstaged by someone young enough to be your grandson.

But others understood the significance of Daniel's gift. Daniel proved that their instincts had been right, in that heaven and earth *can* be connected. They thought that the way to know God was by studying his creation. That was not wrong; it was simply not enough. But now they discovered that the Living God also speaks! A faith based on revelation was not only possible, it was to be found among the Jews. This conviction would survive from generation to generation for over five hundred years, until several of their number followed a heavenly sign, a "star," to the place where heaven would actually come down to earth. We will revisit them later.

Jews were known in the ancient world for many things: their rituals and laws, their sense of community, and tenacity of faith. But Daniel brought to these Gentiles the essence of the Jewish calling. God spoke to them. More than that, the Living God intended to speak *through* them to Gentiles!

And what God said to Nebuchadnezzar was not just some local news. It was God's divine plan for the future. The future of Babylon and other kingdoms, yes. But more than that, the future of God's own restored kingdom on earth. *Nothing of this clarity and magnitude had ever been revealed before.* God chose to reveal it through a young man with the larger faith to embrace God's dream for his life over his own dreams. And God revealed that his dream for Daniel was part of a redemption stretching across empires and spanning centuries to bring salvation to the world.

The Stone that Became a Mountain

Context: Daniel 2:31-40

You saw, O king, and behold, a great image. This image, mighty and of exceeding brightness, stood before you, and its appearance was frightening. The head of this image was of fine gold, its chest and arms of silver, its middle and thighs of bronze, its legs of iron, its feet partly of iron and partly of clay. As you looked, a stone was cut out by no human hand, and it struck the image on its feet of iron and clay, and broke them in pieces. Then the iron, the clay, the bronze, the silver, and the gold, all together were broken in pieces, and became like the chaff of the summer threshing floors; and the wind carried them away, so that not a trace of them could be found. But the stone that struck the image became a great mountain and filled the whole earth. (Daniel 2:31-35)

In a sense, Nebuchadnezzar's dream started out like a fulfillment of his deepest desire. From surviving artifacts, we know that he enjoyed statues of himself. He must have enjoyed the thought of his rule reverberating over the centuries. He dreamed of an unnaturally huge statue, strangely constructed. The head was gold, the chest and arms silver, the thighs bronze, the legs iron and the feet iron mixed with clay. Nebuchadnezzar probably recognized the head as his own. Later, he actually created a statue 90′ high, perhaps to mimic his dream. Impressive.

But in his dream a stone appeared, cut out of the earth as by divine might. The stone smashed the statue's feet, whereupon the entire structure fell apart. In the dream, it disintegrated and blew away with the wind. Meanwhile, the stone which had done the damage grew … and grew. It became a mountain and continued growing until it filled the entire earth.

Daniel prefaced his remarks by clarifying that he had no more inherent wisdom than any other man; he had simply received revelation, a vision from God. But to say such a thing is easy. What came next must have rocked the king's soul. Daniel described the exact dream the king saw. The well-known gods of Babylon did not communicate, let alone know what their worshipers were thinking. The God of the Jews must be special. How else could Daniel know his dream in detail?

But such wonder had to be shelved for the time being, because Daniel went on to explain the meaning of the dream. Not all dreams have meanings we can discern. But when someone speaks for a God who proves that he knows your thoughts, it's probably good to listen.

Future history

What Nebuchadnezzar heard was unlike any dream interpretation he had heard from the Magi. This was not about Babylonian politics or the barley harvest. There was no guidance for his battle strategy or construction plans. In fact, although he and Babylon were featured prominently in the dream, it was not mostly about him or his empire. The perspective was different, bigger. It was a vision from God's perspective and about what God planned to do.

The statue functioned as a kind of timeline, running from the present at the head to the distant future at the feet. This timeline featured four distinct empires, with an indefinite future thereafter. Daniel said that the head of gold represented Babylon and its great King Nebuchadnezzar. The silver chest and arms stood for an "inferior" empire that would one day follow Babylon. The bronze thighs marked where the timeline was dominated by yet another kingdom after the silver, one known for the speed of its conquests and geographical breadth of its rule. After that was a kingdom represented by legs of iron known for its power to crush other kingdoms. Then, a mix of iron and clay for feet implied that the iron kingdom would become brittle, breaking up into an unstable pile of nations, some reflecting the original iron powerhouse and others not so much.

We put such stock in technology that we think of civilization as continually progressing. But judging from the value of the materials from top to bottom, God apparently sees the quality of human culture deteriorating.

In this first vision, the identities of the future kingdoms are not specified. But we will see in later visions that the silver kingdom will be identified as that of the Medes and Persians, the bronze kingdom that of the explosive Greek conquest under Alexander the Great. The Medes and Greeks were at least known by the Babylonians. They had no name for the fourth kingdom, for it did not yet exist as a major player. From our perspective, we can see that it naturally describes what we call the Roman Empire, which split into a collection of uneven nation-states that struggle for dominance to this day.

At the section of the timeline around when the fourth kingdom becomes brittle, the statue is smashed by a stone from heaven.

> In the days of those kings the God of heaven will set up a kingdom that shall never be destroyed, nor shall the kingdom be left to another people. It shall break in pieces all these kingdoms and bring them to an end, and it shall stand forever. (Daniel 2:44)

God has a kingdom, too

Every empire likes to think of itself as the kingdom favored by its chosen god. But when the Lord demonstrated his objective reality by describing that particular dream, he declared something else. The Lord declared that his divine kingdom is distinct from any of the kingdoms of this world. His kingdom remained unknown in the history of the ancient superpowers. But in the days of the fourth human empire, the kingdom of God will be revealed and begin to expand throughout the earth—a stone smashing the timeline to mark its beginning.

So, in this first vision of Daniel, which catapulted him to lifelong fame, we learn that the Creator God, from whom mankind is alienated, plans to institute a kingdom of his own:

- not of this world, but from heaven.
- distinct from any political nation (including Israel).

- taking initial shape before the fourth (Roman) empire crumbles.
- more enduring than any empire.
- expanding over all the earth—into all nations.
- ultimately outliving any other kingdom and setting the stage for eternity

The Magi would take note that while all this became known through revelation, it was a prophecy that could be tracked scientifically, fulfilling their dream of connecting heaven and earth. This multi-generational project would become lost over the span of centuries, except for a few persistent Magi who would actually see it through to the heavenly kingdom's beginning (and be memorialized every Christmas!).

King Nebuchadnezzar was so overwhelmed to receive a *genuine* revelation from God that he exalted Daniel in every way. The knowledge of God's kingdom may arise from Israel, but that kingdom itself would involve the whole world. This was both a warning and a promise for Babylon and every nation to come.

At Daniel's request, the king also promoted Daniel's three friends to positions of leadership. While this would separate the team, their faith had already been firmly established, and they would represent the Living God in the provinces while Daniel did the same in the royal court.

Before moving on, I'd like to point out a biblical detail that I think has been generally overlooked. When one of Jesus' disciples first confessed him as the Christ, the Son of God, Jesus celebrated the occasion by changing the man's name to "stone" (Peter).

Blessed are you, Simon Bar-Jonah! For flesh and blood has not revealed this to you, but my Father who is in heaven. And I tell you, you are Peter, and on this rock I will build my church, and the gates of hell shall not prevail against it. (Matthew 16:17-18)

Centuries of argument about the nature of church authority has had Catholics and Protestants endlessly debating about what "this rock" refers to. Peter himself? His confession? The work of God the Father? But consider the place that Daniel had in the mind of Christ in prophesying the arrival and expansion of God's kingdom. Perhaps Jesus declared that Simon's faith marked the exact moment when Daniel's prophesied stone landed in world history, and despite Satan's opposition that stone would irresistibly grow into a mountain that would fill the whole earth. Something to think about.

God had begun to respond to Daniel's passion for a larger faith by revealing his plan to reinstate his rule across every nation. More revelations would follow that will further specify the arrival and work of Jesus Christ, and the expansion of his worldwide kingdom.

But I See Four Men

Context: Daniel 3:1-30

King Nebuchadnezzar made an image of gold, whose height was sixty cubits and its breadth six cubits. He set it up on the plain of Dura, in the province of Babylon. Then King Nebuchadnezzar sent to gather the satraps, the prefects, and the governors, the counselors, the treasurers, the justices, the magistrates, and all the officials of the provinces to come to the dedication of the image that King Nebuchadnezzar had set up. Then the satraps, the prefects, and the governors, the counselors, the treasurers, the justices, the magistrates, and all the officials of the provinces gathered for the dedication of the image that King Nebuchadnezzar had set up. And they stood before the image that Nebuchadnezzar had set up. And the herald proclaimed aloud, "You are commanded, O peoples, nations, and languages, that when you hear the sound of the horn, pipe, lyre, trigon, harp, bagpipe, and every kind of music, you are to fall down and worship the golden image that King Nebuchadnezzar has set up. And whoever does not fall down and worship shall immediately be cast into a burning fiery furnace." Therefore, as soon as all the peoples heard the sound of the horn, pipe, lyre, trigon, harp, bagpipe, and every kind of music, all the peoples, nations, and languages fell down and worshiped the golden image that King Nebuchadnezzar had set up. (Daniel 3:1-7)

Through the divine revelation of Daniel's dream interpretation, King Nebuchadnezzar had come to believe that the Jewish God was powerful, especially when it came to revealing mysteries. As the years passed, Daniel's three friends were assigned high-level duties in various parts of the empire while Daniel remained at the royal court. The three were reunited at a very special empire-wide event. Since Daniel was apparently not present, we assume that he had to supervise the court while the king traveled to the festivities.

The event was designed to cement the unity of the Babylonian empire under Nebuchadnezzar's reign. The empire included people of different religions. Leaders from many areas, groups and factions were called to gather not far from the capital to celebrate a new monument dedicated to Babylonian glory.

The golden image

The monument was a narrow structure some 90 feet high. It could have been a pillar of flat rock called a stele (pronounced either like "steel" or "stelay"), with engravings of words and images. "Image of gold," however, suggests a high round column with a gold statue at the top. The gold image was meant to be a religious symbol (people were instructed to worship it). It could have been a lion, representing Ishtar, the goddess of fertility, love and war. Nebuchadnezzar set up over a hundred lion images in the entrance to his capital and in his throne room. Alternatively, it could have been a bust of Nebuchadnezzar himself, embodying his part in his divine dream, and focusing on his own royal glory. However it was designed, the monument functioned as a tribute to Babylon's (and Nebuchadnezzar's) first place among earth's empires.

The symbol, therefore, had both religious and political meaning. The empire was polytheistic and people groups were allowed to focus on various gods. But unity demanded that everyone agree to also worship Nebuchadnezzar's chosen god, and therefore recognize his divine authority. The celebration consisted of gathering around this image and, with great fanfare, bowing down to acknowledge Nebuchadnezzar's absolute rule over a diverse empire. To underscore the political nature of this religious test, the king decreed that anyone who refused to bow down would be cast into the huge industrial furnace used in the monument's construction.

Present at the ceremony were Shadrach, Meshach and Abednego, the three friends who stood alongside Daniel in their secret affirmation of the Lord's ultimate sovereignty. They supported Nebuchadnezzar's rule, but they would never give him a place of honor and obedience over Israel's Lord and Savior. When the music hit its crescendo, they found themselves the only men still standing.

Foreign slaves who had been promoted quickly above local leadership could not have been universally loved. "Certain Chaldeans" approached the king with malice to expose the apparent disloyalty of these Jews, reminding the king of his decree to burn such traitors alive. Nebuchadnezzar brought the three before him to make sure they understood what was involved, and gave them an opportunity to demonstrate their loyalty. He wished them no harm, and thought what he was asking was quite reasonable. Nebuchadnezzar had acknowledged the power of their god and was not asking anyone to forsake the gods they preferred. He simply wanted religious agreement that when push came to shove, he was sovereign in all things.

The overlap of religion and politics became crystal clear in the king's last comment, "And who is the god who will deliver you out of my hands?" (vs. 15)—not out of the hands of *my god*, but out of *my* hands. Regardless of what religious image was displayed, it was to the king that everyone bowed.

No

For the three Jewish officers, the question of their worship and ultimate allegiance had already been settled over three years of vegetables. Their conviction had been established, now the only question was whether they would stand by it. They did. "Our God whom we serve is able to deliver us from the burning fiery furnace" (vs. 17). Our God is *able*. But how did they know that God actually *would* save them from the king's furnace? They didn't. Their response to Nebuchadnezzar was essentially a declaration of God's sovereignty. God could save them if that was his will.

But the sovereignty of God was only half of their conviction; the other half was the worthiness of God. So they followed up with, "But if not [if he does not save us], be it known to you, O king, that we will not serve your gods or worship the golden image that you have set up" (vs. 18). Even though they were convinced that God could deliver them, they did not presume that he would. After all, it had been God's will to exile Israel from the Promised Land as punishment for their sins. Their God was powerful enough to save them, but they did not know whether or not that was his will. They were certain, however, that only the Living God was worthy of worship. For them, the Living God ranked higher than any gold lion, or king, or empire. Their heart and soul belonged to him, and they would have no other gods before him.

"Then Nebuchadnezzar was filled with fury, and the expression of his face was changed against Shadrach, Meshach, and Abednego" (vs. 19). For the king of Babylon, religion was not an abstract nicety. Religion could serve several purposes, but its primary purpose was to support his regime. Every faction was welcome to leave that assembly to worship Marduk, Tiamat, Shamash or any of the seven planetary deities, using images of any animal or bird they wanted. But not before they bowed to Nebuchadnezzar's golden image. Not before they bowed before *him*. Not before they pledged their allegiance and loyalty to him above any other claim. And if these three young upstarts couldn't do that, then they would become a lesson no one would ever forget. He ordered the furnace to be fired up, had the three friends bound and ordered for them to be thrown in. The industrial furnace was so hot that the soldiers who threw them in were scorched.

Fellowship in the fire

Nebuchadnezzar got his wish for a display that would never be forgotten, but not in the way he expected. We learn what happened through the wide-eyed witness of Nebuchadnezzar himself.

Then King Nebuchadnezzar was astonished and rose up in haste. He declared to his counselors, "Did we not cast three men bound into the fire?" They answered and said to the king, "True, O king." He answered and said, "But I see four men unbound, walking in the midst of the fire, and they are not hurt; and the appearance of the fourth is like a son of the gods." (Daniel 3:24-25)

With Daniel, Nebuchadnezzar had witnessed a miracle of knowledge in the revelation of his dream. Now he beheld a physical miracle of power. Had he been told of it, he probably would not have believed it. But he saw it with his own eyes. When Shadrach, Meshack and Abednego emerged unscathed from the fire not even smelling of smoke, Nebuchadnezzar was once again faced with the reality and sovereignty of the God of Israel.

What happened shocked and deeply moved him. He believed that Israel's Lord was a revealer of mysteries (every god did something, after all). But Israel's God could not have much in the power department because Babylon had torn down the Lord's capital city and destroyed his Temple. Daniel and his friends heard the Lord's prophets predict Israel's defeat as the Lord's own doing, so for the four of them, Babylon's victory only underscored the Lord's power. But Nebuchadnezzar did not follow Israelite prophets. He needed something more direct and visceral. Seeing men calmly walking out of a blazing furnace was something he would never forget. Neither has anyone since who is familiar with the Old Testament.

What of the fourth man in the furnace? Surprisingly, nothing more is ever said about him. Since the Jewish men proclaimed that their God would deliver them if it were his will, Nebuchadnezzar, and we, must assume that the fourth man was some manifestation of God's presence. An angel? A pre-incarnate vision of Christ? The king clearly identified him as an angel (vs. 28), but since the term "angel" could refer to either a supernatural or human being, we simply do not know what Nebuchadnezzar thought he saw. What we do know is how Nebuchadnezzar responded to what he saw:

> Therefore I make a decree: Any people, nation, or language that speaks anything against the God of Shadrach, Meshach, and Abednego shall be torn limb from limb, and their houses laid in ruins, for there is no other god who is able to rescue in this way. (Daniel 3:29)

King Nebuchadnezzar had never encountered a god who bested his military might. But the one he only knew as "the God of Shadrach, Meshack and Abednego" apparently had supreme power to save those faithful to him.

Civil religion

Devout Christians and Jews who read this story are, of course, drawn to the wonderful faithfulness of Shadrach, Meshack and Abednego, but it is also worth noting that popular religion is still typically as much about politics as it is about faith. In every culture, approved religions support the state. This is true the world over and across the centuries. There is either an explicit or tacit agreement between favored religions (or ideologies), and those who politically rule. The state usually finds ways to subsidize favored religion in exchange for receiving its blessing and support.

The Book of Revelation describes this relationship in a striking picture of how the fallen world works. "Then I saw another beast rising out of the earth. It had two horns like a lamb and it spoke like a dragon ... and makes the earth and its inhabitants worship the first beast" (Revelation 13:11-12). The first "beast" represents an amalgam of state power (combining all the beasts in Chapter 7 of Daniel), while the second beast serves as a "false prophet" that claims divine insight and directs its followers to worship the political powers that be. This visionary representation works for most, if not all, nations and empires. Religion is one of the standard ways that leaders maintain their power.

This chapter of Daniel illustrates this dynamic in action. Nebuchadnezzar commanded every segment of his empire to gather for a religious ceremony. The details of the golden image are not mentioned, because it didn't really matter. The king raised the image as a uniting religious symbol of the empire, and he expected everyone to acknowledge it as such. We noted above that the true and obvious point of the bowing was political, that is, to submit to Nebuchadnezzar ("and who is the god who will deliver you out of *my* hands?") Therefore, the purpose of the religious ceremony was to ensure that every religion or ideology represented in the empire acknowledged the king as a superior authority to their chosen religion. The consequences of asserting spiritual autonomy: death.

The struggle between the kingdom of God and the kingdoms of this world is a great theme of Daniel, emerging in his very first dream interpretation. The point of this chapter is not only that God rewards personal faith, but that God's people must always be prepared to worship God above any state or ruler or institution. The commitment to do so, in any such context, will always be a risky business. The three Jews were not in any way opposed to Nebuchadnezzar or his policies. The three

Jews were not trying to push their own agenda. They were simply adamant that when push comes to shove, God has first claim to their allegiance, not the state.

The ceremony of the golden idol illustrates this challenge in its starkest form. Nebuchadnezzar was not asking for any specific obedience. The king even liked these three nonconformists (because of their former history), and went out of his way to explain things. The king did not ask for any particular compromise, and he assured his continued favor and reward for good service. But he insisted that everyone understand that when the king *does* require obedience—even if goes against their spiritual conscience—everyone *will* submit. The ceremony required a promise of unconditional loyalty, promised state benefits in return, and threatened state sanctions for non-compliance. It was equivalent to the token ceremonial toast to Caesar as Lord, which the first Christians declined at the cost of their property and lives.

But even at this early stage of Daniel's story, his three friends were already equipped to face this challenge. This is true for two reasons, and it is important that we understand them both. First, they had formed a settled commitment to put God first no matter what. Shadrach, Meshack and Abednego did not naturally jump to radical obedience when faced with imminent death; they had already practiced this decision over a thousand meals of vegetables until it shaped their identity. The First Commandment (which leads to all the others) defined who they were. They were worshipers of the Lord God, the Living God, and they simply would not worship anything or anyone above him.

But they were also equipped in another way, a way that had to do with their goals in life. The children of

Abraham had been chosen by God to be his vehicle to redeem the entire world. Through the exodus and his commandments, God revealed what redemption means: reconciliation with the God we have offended, reconciliation with other people we have mistreated, and reconciliation with our role of caring for Creation. Israel was called to be a light to the Gentiles as they discovered God's covenant with Abraham and saw its impact in real lives.

The Babylonian captivity highlighted Israel's failure. From their small personal perspective, Shadrach, Meshack and Abednego must have wondered if Israel's mission could ever be fulfilled. But Daniel's vision saw the kingdom of God scripted to appear in force hundreds of years in the future. Israel would not fail in its mission. That vision enabled them to see the progress of God's kingdom from the perspective of God's throne, a huge plan spanning many nations and many lifetimes. And this perspective was divinely inspired—Daniel had known Nebuchadnezzar's dream! Therefore, it didn't matter when they lived on the timeline of God's plan— whether they died that day or decades later from old age. All that mattered was that they were connected by faith to God's eternal plan. All that mattered was being faithful, regardless of the immediate consequences.

Because of their practiced conviction to not be one of the king's men but to worship God alone, and because of Daniel's vision that gave historical perspective to their place in God's kingdom, they could say words which will be remembered until the kingdoms of this world become the kingdom of our God, words that bear repeating:

> Our God whom we serve is able to deliver us from the burning fiery furnace, and he will deliver us out of your hand, O king. But if not, be it known to you, O king, that we will not serve your gods or worship the golden image that you have set up. (Daniel 3:17-18)

Perhaps these words would be remembered even if Nebuchadnezzar's execution had been successful. But to underscore the importance of their conviction and their perspective, the Lord God did something extraordinary. As the king watched, these three men walked inside the giant furnace as if the flames did not exist. It must have looked as if they were immune to the flames, immune to Nebuchadnezzar's condemnation, immune to *any* condemnation.

Because they were.

The fourth man

> Did we not cast three men bound into the fire? ... But I see four men unbound, walking in the midst of the fire, and they are not hurt; and the appearance of the fourth is like a son of the gods. (Daniel 3:24-25)

The reason these men could not be condemned had to do with the fourth man. Why did the king refer to him as "a son of the gods"? Perhaps because Shadrach, Meshack and Abednego had chosen to stand with their God, and now it was apparent that their God was standing with them. This divine-human figure could have appeared outside of the furnace and quenched the flames, or appeared in Nebuchadnezzar's face to stop the execution. Instead, he chose to identify with those who were condemned, share their condemnation, as it were.

And with him experiencing the fire personally, the flames had no authority over his people. Christians will easily see here a foreshadow of how the Son of God would one day take the place of sinners and bear their condemnation on the cross that they might be spared.

Nebuchadnezzar's faith in the Living God of Israel moved up a few notches. Before, he saw this God as a revealer of mysteries. Now, he calls him, "the Most High God" with amazing power, and the king forbade any blasphemy against him. Moreover, the king promoted the three Jewish leaders even higher, probably to the chagrin of whoever had excitedly pointed out their behavior to the king in the first place.

We are still only three chapters into the Book of Daniel, and already see how the Lord's people can survive and thrive in a world alienated from God. We have seen the power of practiced conviction that shapes our sense of who we are. And we have seen the power of a divine perspective of history. The thought that God has literally orchestrated the history of empires in the past is convincing evidence that he is doing so today, and shall do so until Christ's return. Shadrach, Meshach and Abednego show us that the best course is to link our good to God's glory, our purpose to God's purpose, our story to his story, and be faithful, no matter what.

We have also seen how even the best empires are alienated from God. Nebuchadnezzar was blessed with an amazing dream of the world's future featuring the expansion of God's rule throughout the earth. But his response was to exalt that part of the vision that referenced him (the golden head), twisting it into a civil religion exalting himself. Human power structures always tend toward this. Throughout redemptive history, all cultures will to some extent put God's people at odds with civil leadership's manipulation of religion. We will always be expected to bow to the state image of choice. The civil powers-that-be will even try to degrade biblical religion into an idol that supports them. This is an ongoing test of the faith, identity and purpose of the people of God in any generation.

Humanity was intelligently designed to function as the image of God in this world, reflecting his wisdom and his love. But alienation from our Creator has diminished our capacity. Humanity has, in effect, become something less, something that in God's eyes must appear sub-human, and nowhere is this beast-like character seen more vividly than in our institutions of power. In fact, this association of human rule with beasts will drive Daniel's later visions, as God continues to reveal the future history of redemption.

The Most High

Context: Daniel 4:1-37

I saw in the visions of my head as I lay in bed, and behold, a watcher, a holy one, came down from heaven. He proclaimed aloud and said thus: "Chop down the tree and lop off its branches, strip off its leaves and scatter its fruit. Let the beasts flee from under it and the birds from its branches. But leave the stump of its roots in the earth, bound with a band of iron and bronze, amid the tender grass of the field. Let him be wet with the dew of heaven. Let his portion be with the beasts in the grass of the earth. Let his mind be changed from a man's, and let a beast's mind be given to him; and let seven periods of time pass over him. The sentence is by the decree of the watchers, the decision by the word of the holy ones, to the end that the living may know that the Most High rules the kingdom of men and gives it to whom he will and sets over it the lowliest of men." (Daniel 4:13-17)

Merriam-Webster defines insanity as "unsoundness of mind or lack of the ability to understand." Human beings are distinct from every other creature, in part because of our ability to consciously find meaning in our world. We excel at perceiving relationships, categories, and cause and effect. Non-human mammals, the "beasts" of the Bible, have a rudimentary intelligence, but humans uniquely comprehend reality in terms of meaning and purpose, values and ethics. When people lose those abilities, we call it "insanity." In some ways, it is like becoming a beast.

Nebuchadnezzar certainly considered himself sane, being "at ease in my house and prospering in my palace" (vs. 4). Babylon was the world's greatest empire. In his first interpreted dream, the Most High himself classified future empires as inferior. And who was responsible for this glory? The king, of course. When Nebuchadnezzar dreamed of a great statue with a golden head, that head represented him. And wasn't it one of his conquered retainers whom the Most High used to interpret the dream? True, his order to execute the three Jews was overturned by divine action, but wasn't that a sign that graced his eyes? Wasn't he the one to see a son of god walking in the flames? (Perhaps it takes greatness to see greatness.) The world moves in the wake of its great leaders, its course set by their vision. The world is the stage of great empires that exist for the glory of man, and especially those most successful of men ...

Or so Nebuchadnezzar believed.

The danger of pride

A change in the king's perspective began, as before, with a dream—another dream which troubled him greatly. As usual, he petitioned the wise men on duty for an explanation. When they failed, he turned again for help to the Hebrew, Belteshazzar (Daniel). By the way he speaks to Daniel, it is clear that the king still worships Marduk as chief among the gods, although he has come to greatly admire Daniel's God as a powerful revealer of mysteries.

In his first dream, Nebuchadnezzar saw a great statue that was smashed. This time, he saw a great tree.

> The tree grew and became strong, and its top reached to heaven, and it was visible to the end of the whole earth. Its leaves were beautiful and its fruit abundant, and in it was food for all. The beasts of the field found shade under it, and the birds of the heavens lived in its branches, and all flesh was fed from it. (Daniel 4:11-12)

This time, instead of seeing a great statue smashed, he sees a great tree chopped down and stripped of its leaves and fruit. The animals that had found shelter in it are scattered, and the stump is bound with chains. Even in the dream, it is clear to Nebuchadnezzar that the stump represents a person. This person's mind degenerates into that of a beast—he does not turn into a beast, but begins to think like one for a period of time. The purpose of this is stated in the dream, "that the living may know that the Most High rules the kingdom of men and gives it to whom he will and sets over it the lowliest of men."

Daniel seems hesitant to share his interpretation. When pressed, he states, "My lord, may the dream be for those who hate you and its interpretation for your enemies!" He then goes on to explain that the tree represents Nebuchadnezzar personally. His earthly glory is unmatched. But he shall be humbled with insanity, eating grass and sleeping outside at night like an ox. This shall last for a set period of time, after which Nebuchadnezzar will acknowledge that it is the God of Heaven, and not himself, who ultimately rules the kingdom of men. After this, both his sanity and position will be restored.

At this point, Daniel does something unusual for a court retainer. He gives the king unsolicited counsel. In doing this, Daniel imitated the prophets of Israel, who often called their kings to repentance and faith. Nebuchadnezzar's dream was a picture of coming chastisement for his unbounded pride. Perhaps this madness could be avoided if the king acknowledged his sin by practicing righteousness and showing mercy to the oppressed.

There is no record of Nebuchadnezzar's immediate response to Daniel's exhortation. It is worth noting that the dream did not become reality for a full year. It is unclear whether this delay implies a half-hearted attempt at repentance on the king's part or an extra measure of grace on God's.

A man or a beast?

One year later, King Nebuchadnezzar's pride is again in full bloom. Daniel remembers him walking on the roof of his palace, saying, "Is not this great Babylon, which I have built by my mighty power as a royal residence and for the glory of my majesty?" (vs. 30). This one sentence summarizes Nebuchadnezzar's self-obsession. (To illustrate: he used some 15 million bricks in his building projects, and almost all of them were individually imprinted with his name and claim to greatness.)

As Nebuchadnezzar spoke, he was interrupted by a voice from heaven declaring that the things pictured in his previous dream would now be fulfilled. He would go mad, imagining himself a beast, and would be excluded from power until he was prepared to acknowledge his rule as a gift from the Most High. Before this season of madness passed, "his hair grew as long as eagles' feathers, and his nails were like bird's claws" (vs. 33).

Especially since this insanity was not permanent, one does not expect much of an historical record of such an indignity. Nevertheless, there are at least two ancient references to consider outside the Book of Daniel. The fourth century AD historian, Eusebius, quoted a history of the Assyrians containing a fourth century BC report that Nebuchadnezzar experienced an unspecified calamity after being "possessed by a foreign god." There is also a Babylonian cuneiform tablet with a broken message that appears to relate how, for a time, Nebuchadnezzar was unwilling or unable to fulfill his role as king.[1]

Americans do not have to look far to appreciate how the illness of leaders is covered up while they are active. One has only to think of President Wilson's stroke or President Roosevelt's polio.

Rediscovering what it means to be human

In time, the king's reason returned. As he put it,

> I blessed the Most High, and praised and honored him who lives forever, for his dominion is an everlasting dominion, and his kingdom endures from generation to generation; all the inhabitants of the earth are accounted as nothing, and he does according to his will among the host of heaven and among the inhabitants of the earth; and none can stay his hand or say to him, "What have you done?" (Daniel 4:34-35)

---

[1] See "The Madness of King Nebuchadnezzar," posted on biblereadingarcheology.com by Keith Paterson on September 25, 2017.

Babylon's leaders reaffirmed Nebuchadnezzar's authority, and the king emerged from the experience convinced that the Most High's power and authority does indeed supersede any human king or kingdom.

It is worth noting that Nebuchadnezzar's reign was not all about the glories of conquest and monuments. He apparently responded to his affliction by taking Daniel's exhortation to heart. In his forty-three years as king, artistic achievements blessed both rich and poor, schools and libraries flourished, Babylonian culture became less tied to their old gods, and women were raised to a status with nearly equal rights as men.

Nebuchadnezzar's madness is much more than an interesting anecdote in Daniel's memoirs. It underscores not only God's superior power and authority, but also the superiority of his character, which we were made to reflect, but do not. Genesis describes the Living God creating mankind with intelligence and empathy. These combine in the human conscience to create a fundamental awareness of good and evil, especially in relation to treating others as we wish to be treated. The Apostle Paul describes the conscience as a natural element of human life, independent of any any biblical knowledge (Romans 1:18-2:11). If conscience were the only factor, human beings would honor their Designer and enjoy pursuing his design. This relationship with God and with each other describes the "kingdom" God intended for humanity on Planet Earth.

In this account of Nebuchadnezzar's madness, we have an historical caricature of sin as human insanity. If, indeed, mankind was created to love God and love one another, it would be insane to either 1) pretend to dethrone God and grant ourselves ultimate authority and glory, or 2) oppress others by expanding our influence and options at others' expense. Daniel points out how Nebuchadnezzar was guilty on both these counts. Daniel's interpretation points out Nebuchadnezzar's pride, and then offers an admonition to practice righteousness and forsake oppression. The king was reduced to beastliness because dominating others as if you are God is a *sub-human* thing to do, something far less than what we are capable of and what we were made for. It is when Nebuchadnezzar honors the Living God and is prepared to care for his citizens that he becomes the most human.

It would be a mistake to assume God always humbles the prideful and oppressive today, for that would assume the kingdom of God is currently active in its fullness. Given the first dream of the smashed stature, we know that the kingdom of God is something that will grow slowly over time, out of Israel and into every nation, culminating with final judgment. Nevertheless, Nebuchadnezzar stands as a striking object lesson.

Chapter 4 of Daniel introduces the idea that, through its leaders, a nation can become sub-human. Later chapters will show that this was not only true of Nebuchadnezzar's rule. It is the way God sees every kingdom alienated from him.

Weighed in the Balances

Context: Daniel 5:1-31

Then from his presence the hand was sent, and this writing was inscribed. And this is the writing that was inscribed: MENE, MENE, TEKEL, and PARSIN. This is the interpretation of the matter: MENE, God has numbered the days of your kingdom and brought it to an end; TEKEL, you have been weighed in the balances and found wanting; PERES, your kingdom is divided and given to the Medes and Persians. (Daniel 5:24-28)

When torn from his home, family and culture, young Daniel and his friends resolved to remain faithful to the Living God of Abraham and Moses. They chose to believe his prophets, who predicted and explained Jerusalem's downfall as the chastisement of God on a people unfaithful to their calling to be his light in the world. Daniel's great desire was to be faithful to the Lord, and to understand how what was happening would work into his greater plan. God's deliverance of these men confirmed their faithfulness, and the visions given to Daniel describe the coming of God's kingdom and the tribulations that would accompany its world-wide expansion.

Chapter 5 moves on from Nebuchadnezzar's reign to that of his son, Nabonidus. Nabonidus himself does not appear in this story. Secular history tells us he was out fighting Babylon's battles, battles for glory and expansion in Arabia, and battles to survive closer to home. Local affairs were managed by his son, Belshazzar, essentially a co-regent who ruled in his father's name.

The ~~right~~ wrong stuff

Belshazzar was a man who enjoyed his wine and liked to party. Daniel describes a huge party of a thousand guests where wine flowed freely. We have no idea what the occasion was. What made it strange was the timing. While Nabonidus fought on the frontier, two factions of the existing empire had combined forces to foment rebellion. Nabonidus was forced to return to Babylon to defend the capital city. Given what our text says happened the very next day, it's clear that Nabonidus had just lost what we know was a decisive battle about 50 miles north of the city. Why the party? Was Belshazzar in denial? Had he not yet received word of the defeat? What an inappropriate time for a party.

But it got worse. To have enough vessels for everyone to drink, Belshazzar ordered that vessels from the looted Jerusalem Temple be brought out and distributed to his lords, wives and concubines. They used those vessels to drink to the honor of their gods. It is hard to imagine a greater offense to the God of Heaven.

As they worshiped their idols using the Lord's holy vessels, the Lord responded with a message. Among the items taken from the Temple and brought out for the party was a golden lampstand. A hand appeared and wrote on the plaster wall illuminated by the lampstand.

Belshazzar almost collapsed—not because of the message, but because of the supernatural appearance of the writing.

The message itself seemed unintelligible. Our Bible reads, "Mene, Mene, Tekel, and Parsin." Their language had no written vowels, but only consonants. Vowels were implied by the context and would determine, for example, whether these words were nouns or verbs. Taken as nouns, these were words for coins used both as money and also as weights in a balance (think of a similar dual meaning of the English "pound"). What did it all mean?

As was the custom, the king called upon his Magi, or Wise Men, to answer the riddle, promising wealth and power to whoever succeeded. Of course, none were able, since the meaning depended on a context in the mind of God. This failure greatly alarmed the king. God had spoken, but no one knew what he meant because no one knew his mind.

The queen apparently knew more about the Magi than her husband, for she suggested that he call upon Daniel, who in times past had demonstrated to Nebuchadnezzar the ability to understand God's mind. In her words, "an excellent spirit, knowledge, and understanding to interpret dreams, explain riddles, and solve problems were found in this Daniel." Daniel was called, and the king explained the situation, promising again great wealth and power for an explanation.

Those who do not learn from history …

Daniel notably tells this poor excuse of a king to keep his gifts, although he will interpret the message. Since the key to the interpretation is knowing the context, Daniel rehearses the entire story of Nebuchadnezzar's pride toward God and oppression toward people. He describes the divine chastisement that reduced the former king to the life of a beast, and how he was restored when he gave glory to God and urged everyone to honor the God of Heaven who has revealed himself to the Jews. That was the context. Apparently, Belshazzar had learned nothing from this. He was as proud and arrogant as his grandfather.

> … you have lifted up yourself against the Lord of heaven. And the vessels of his house have been brought in before you, and you and your lords, your wives, and your concubines have drunk wine from them. And you have praised the gods of silver and gold, of bronze, iron, wood, and stone, which do not see or hear or know, but the God in whose hand is your breath, and whose are all your ways, you have not honored. (Daniel 5:23)

The context interprets the message. It was not a string of *nouns*, but rather *verbs* meaning "to number," "to weigh" and "to divide." Daniel unpacks the message as:

> MENE, God has numbered the days of your kingdom and brought it to an end; TEKEL, you have been weighed in the balances and found wanting; PERES, your kingdom is divided and given to the Medes and Persians. (Daniel 5:26-28)

Actually, that last part about the kingdom being given to the Medes and Persians had already happened, for the key battle had already been lost.

Belshazzar fulfilled his promise to shower Daniel with wealth and power. But the next day, Belshazzar himself was killed and the kingdom taken over by Darius the Mede. We don't know if Darius heard about Daniel's prediction. But we do know that Daniel was so valued that he was kept on by the new administration.

It's a jungle out there

The handwriting on the wall essentially parallels Nebuchadnezzar's dream of the great tree. When filled with pride and oppression, human society becomes sub-human, preferring to worship idols we create (thus worshiping ourselves) rather than worshiping our Creator.

But this account takes us one step further in preparing us for the astounding visions to come. It's not only Nebuchadnezzar who ruled in a sub-human manner; his successor Belshazzar made the same mistake. So would the next king from the Medes. In fact, *all* of this world's empires and kingdoms are more or less bestial.

This is not to say that every kingdom is equal. Daniel's first vision displayed a series of kingdoms of differing glory. Kingdoms differ in the way one type of animal differs from another—there is a big difference between a majestic golden eagle and a monster with iron teeth, ten horns and feet that crush its prey.

But *all* human kingdoms are beasts, in the simple sense that they are not what God designed for humanity, and are, therefore, sub-human. This is just as true for China's Ming Dynasty, Austria's Habsburgs, England's Tutors, or any American administration. If a kingdom's leaders gather power over time, they will more or less follow Nebuchadnezzar's pride and willingness to oppress. America's remarkable Constitution is all about constraining political power with checks and balances and a Bill of Rights, but we have seen that it only works when people want it to. There are times when the United States has, indeed, been a noble, high-flying eagle. But it is still a beast, and its nature can change very quickly.

The world needs redemption. It needs a Savior. It needs the kingdom of God to be restored. And after one more test of his faith, Daniel would be given a grand view of God's salvation plan such as no one else had ever seen.

The Lion's Den

Context: Daniel 6:1-28

Then the king commanded, and Daniel was brought and cast into the den of lions. The king declared to Daniel, "May your God, whom you serve continually, deliver you!" And a stone was brought and laid on the mouth of the den, and the king sealed it with his own signet and with the signet of his lords, that nothing might be changed concerning Daniel. Then the king went to his palace and spent the night fasting; no diversions were brought to him, and sleep fled from him.
Then, at break of day, the king arose and went in haste to the den of lions. As he came near to the den where Daniel was, he cried out in a tone of anguish. The king declared to Daniel, "O Daniel, servant of the living God, has your God, whom you serve continually, been able to deliver you from the lions?" Then Daniel said to the king, "O king, live forever! My God sent his angel and shut the lions' mouths, and they have not harmed me, because I was found blameless before him; and also before you, O king, I have done no harm." (Daniel 6:16-22)

During Nebuchadnezzar's test of submission at his great religious statue, Shadrach, Meshack and Abednego demonstrated that they would not compromise their faith in the Living God's supremacy. They were committed to serve the king well, but never to exalt him above God. For their integrity, they were thrown into an industrial furnace. God intervened, and convinced Nebuchadnezzar that there is a Most High God in heaven.

Daniel missed all that. We assume that he had to remain in the capital to keep the government running. Nebuchadnezzar learned from the experience, and never tested people in that way again. But the new kingdom of the Medes and Persians had taken over. This chapter demonstrates that questions about civil loyalty and faith are fundamental to every administration.

No one is exempt from trial

Daniel had risen quickly in Darius' court. Darius[1] came to trust in him so much that he appointed Daniel one of three officials over the 120 local governors. Daniel had a reputation for having "an excellent spirit" and became a favorite of Darius. In fact, the word was that Daniel was about to be promoted yet again, this time to prominence among the three.

This prompted the same kind of reaction that was directed against Shadrach, Meshack and Abednego. Local Babylonian leaders became envious of Daniel's success, and were probably none too keen about serving under a Jew. They were at first stymied as to how to remove him, since he had earned a sterling reputation for faithfulness and competency. Then they realized that he was even more careful in his devotion to "the law of his God." The first law, or commandment, was that he could have no

---

[1] Darius may be a title or the original name Daniel knew for the Mede leader who took the name Cyrus when he ascended to the throne.

gods before the Lord, and that, they hoped, would be the key to his downfall.

Their plan combined an appeal to vanity, some thinly veiled blackmail, and downright falsehood. They approached King Darius with a suggestion that his new reign be cemented with a great show of loyalty that illustrated how every segment of the empire, including every religion, was subservient to him above all. This was precisely what Nebuchadnezzar had tried to do earlier. Except this time, the idea came from Darius' "devoted" retainers. Instead of bowing before a golden idol (which would require a huge effort to assemble leaders), this time all that was suggested was to require people to bring their petitions to Darius only, and not to their own gods, for one month.

This was hardly a serious piece of legislation. It would have been completely unenforcible. The empire was vast; there was no way to keep track of everyone's prayers. And prayers can be thought, not spoken. But this was not meant to be serious legislation. It really only involved the high officials, as a show of unity, and (this is where the falsehood came in) they reported that they were *unanimous* in their suggestion, implying that Daniel had signed off on it. In essence, they claimed to speak for everyone requesting a "King Darius Month" as a show of national unity.

The clever part was asking for a written decree. Once signed, this temporary declaration gained the status of law. American Presidents have made many proclamations setting months aside for worthy purposes, like National Arts & Humanities Month (October), or African-American Music Appreciation Month (June), or even National Ice Cream Month (July). But there is nothing that is binding to such proclamations; they are about national unity and promoting a president's popularity. Making "Darius First" month a law was unnecessary, but played to the king's vanity. It also assured Daniel's destruction, or so they thought. The reputation of the laws of the Medes and the Persians was that they could not be revoked. Of course the king could revoke a law, but that would be a huge embarrassment if people found out (hence the implied blackmail).

Trial exposes our true convictions

Daniel's response to this decree was to ignore it, not out of disrespect for Darius but out of a greater respect for God. Daniel used the highest chamber of his house for prayer. His practice was to open the windows that faced toward Jerusalem and pray to God three times a day. He had done so for years, and everyone knew it. The day he heard of the decree, he changed nothing. He could have gone a month without praying, or simply closed his windows when he prayed, or prayed silently at night. But he did none of that. His enemies could clearly see and perhaps hear him praying as usual—now in direct violation of a royal decree.

They ran like schoolchildren tattling on a classmate, telling Darius how naughty Daniel was. Except that this game was for keeps. Darius was dismayed. He must have been inwardly angry to have been made a fool like that, and his anger would come back upon these plotters. But his immediate concern was to seek a way to save his favorite administrator and Magi. But there was no way to do that without displaying his foolishness for all to see.

As Darius relented and had Daniel brought to the lions, he commended Daniel's life to his God, hoping that somehow he would survive. A stone closed the entrance to the lion's den, and Daniel was sealed inside until daybreak. Darius' attitude is seen in how he kept awake all night hoping for Daniel's deliverance, and he was overjoyed to find Daniel unharmed in the morning.

Once Daniel was secure, the king turned his attention to the men who played him for a fool. He made certain that they suffered the exact fate they had wished on Daniel. Darius then wrote a proclamation for the whole empire declaring Daniel's God to the true and Living God, whose kingdom will never end and who works wonders for those who trust him.

We know that Daniel and the lion's den shows how God takes care of those who put him first. Here are two other observations worth considering:

First, Daniel suffered trials in spite of his strong faith. Probably every Christian would like to think that if our faith is strong and we serve God well, God will reward us by sparing us trials. It's natural to want this, even though Jesus clearly said, "Blessed are those who are persecuted because of righteousness, for theirs is the kingdom of heaven" (Matthew 5:10). Paul added "In fact, everyone who wants to live a godly life in Christ Jesus will be persecuted" (2 Timothy 3:12). Daniel served his nation in exemplary fashion. He earned the good will of the king. His enemies could not charge him with any true offense. When condemned, he did not criticize the king or his ruling. Neither did he attack those who attacked him. He did not try to obey God secretly. He did everything right … and he was still attacked and condemned to death. Such things do not reflect the kingdom of God, but we also live in one of the kingdoms of this world, where they happen all the time.

Faith and politics

The other thing that is clear is that the religious attack on Daniel was really all about power, not religion. Most religious attacks have little to do with religion. It's hard to find any religious extremism that is not rooted in political conflict.

Think about it. While it involved a different king and a different situation, the challenge to Daniel covered the same ground as the incident with his three friends and the fiery furnace years earlier. As power concentrates in any kingdom of this world, the issue of ultimate loyalty and submission becomes more critical. A nation still committed to "of the people, by the people and for the people" will attempt to guard religious freedom. But the more that a nation becomes "of the leaders, by the leaders and for the leaders," it will insist that every person and every institution show deference to government authorities. For Christians, the first classic historic example was Rome, which heartily encouraged religious freedom—as long as every religion tolerated the Emperor cult and every individual made a token sacrifice acknowledging Caesar as (ultimate) Lord.

Governments may be atheistic, agnostic or even profoundly religious (including nominally Christian). But as power concentrates, it doesn't matter. Atheism, agnosticism and religion are all spun in such a way as to cement central power. Totalitarian regimes don't care about atheism, or agnosticism, or religion; at least they don't care as much about them as maintaining and expanding power. That's what sinful people do, and apart from God's grace we all tend to do such things when given the chance.

This makes the trials of Daniel and his friends perpetually relevant for Christians. Nobody else really cares what Christians do or believe as long as our faith is either invisible or openly supportive of the state. "Supporting the state" does not mean offering private prayers; it means public praise, voting the party line, and compliance with whatever institutional leaders consider important. Mature Christians will be properly patriotic and politically involved. But totalitarian rulers insist that Christians make patriotism and party politics more important than God's law or following Jesus. Christians are usually tolerated and may even receive perks (remember the king's food) as long as they praise the right ideology, affirm whatever the authorities say and submit to whatever the authorities demand. When they refuse, totalitarian governments push back and push hard.

Daniel was not in trouble because he was a rebel, and he was not in trouble simply because he was a Jew. He got in trouble because he refused to put civil authorities before God.

The text actually makes it quite clear that Daniel's attack was not religiously motivated. It was motivated by his rivals' desire for power. Religion was simply a tool used by the conspirators to hide their lust for advancement. As governments become more bestial, they may actually make religion more prominent, but only as a tool of influence to gain yet more power. In the Christian perspective, putting God first is a matter of righteousness, so we would say that we are persecuted for righteousness' sake. But our persecutors are motivated neither by righteousness nor religion; they simply see us as potential obstacles to their control.

And we should note in passing that the same dynamic is true for all religious or ideological minorities. Any Jew, Muslim, Buddhist or Hindu who puts his or her faith first will be persecuted by any totalitarian government. It's not an exclusively "anti-Christian" thing; it's a power thing. That's why so-called "Christian" tyrants also persecute minorities. Genuine Christians should oppose *all* such persecution, no matter who it is aimed against. It is wrong. And, by the way, we will be next.

One Like a Son of Man

Context: Daniel 7:1-28

> I saw in the night visions, and behold, with the clouds of heaven there came one like a son of man, and he came to the Ancient of Days and was presented before him. And to him was given dominion and glory and a kingdom, that all peoples, nations, and languages should serve him; his dominion is an everlasting dominion, which shall not pass away, and his kingdom one that shall not be destroyed.
>
> As for me, Daniel, my spirit within me was anxious, and the visions of my head alarmed me. I approached one of those who stood there and asked him the truth concerning all this. So he told me and made known to me the interpretation of the things. "These four great beasts are four kings who shall arise out of the earth. But the saints of the Most High shall receive the kingdom and possess the kingdom forever, forever and ever." (Daniel 7:13-18)

The Book of Daniel begins with Daniel as a young man and ends when he is old, but it is not presented entirely as a chronology. The narrative of Daniel 7 goes back in time before Daniel 5, early in Belshazzar's regency. There are several theories as to the intended literary pattern of Daniel, but the end result is that the reader can naturally perceive the progression of revelation in Daniel's visions.

The first vision (Daniel 2) portrayed a succession of four kingdoms—unnamed, though it was understood that Babylon was first. At the end of that succession, God's kingdom came to earth from heaven, to eventually expand over all the earth.

The second vision (Daniel 4) portrayed Nebuchadnezzar, leader of the first kingdom in this progression, as a beast because he pridefully exalted himself above the Living God.

The third vision (Daniel 5) declared the successors to Nebuchadnezzar to be as prideful as he was. Pride is not just a personal failing of one leader, but a huge temptation for all who wield extreme power.

Putting it all together

This fourth vision in Daniel 7 combines these ideas. We have the same succession of kingdoms that ends with the appearance of God's kingdom. This time, however, *all* the earthly empires are depicted as beasts (vs. 17), all energized by a pride that claims the right to rule like God over their citizens. The kingdoms are still unnamed, though once again, there is a clear identification of the first beast/kingdom, since the winged lion was an established image for Babylon.

As to the other kingdoms, it is not yet clear who they are. But peeking ahead one chapter, we know that the voracious bear is the kingdom that succeeded Babylon (Medes/Persian). The four headed leopard depicts the startlingly swift conquest of Alexander the Great, whose empire settled into four segments. The most interesting is the fourth monster beast.

It was different from all the former beasts, and it had ten horns. While I was thinking about the horns, there before me was another horn, a little one, which came up among them; and three of the first horns were uprooted before it. This horn had eyes like the eyes of a man and a mouth that spoke boastfully. (Daniel 7:7-8)

Daniel could not have understood these details. We, however, can look back on how the future Roman Republic would come together from ten provinces, merge under the shared rule of a three person triumvirate, who were replaced by one, Augustus, who then declared himself divine.

It is also worth noting that the beasts emerge from the sea. Whatever that meant to Daniel, it is a motif that will be repeated in the Book of Revelation. There, the characteristics of all four beasts will be combined into one (Revelation 13:1-2), representing generically the kingdoms of this world in rebellion against the Living God.

We see in verses 16-18 that the pattern of Daniel 2 is repeated: four successive kingdoms—beastly, prideful, sub-human kingdoms of this world—will be followed by the arrival of God's kingdom on earth, which will displace the others and reign eternally under a fully human king. The other thing specifically stated is that it would be during the time of the single horn that the kingdom of God would be manifest (as Luke later records in the New Testament, in the days of Caesar Augustus).

It's also worth noting here the first occurrence of an unusual measurement, "a time, times and half a time" (vs. 25). Beginning with the appearance of God's kingdom during the fourth worldly kingdom before it breaks apart, there will be a difficult period for God's people lasting three and a half "times." There is no explanation given as to why a specific time interval is not given. That will await Daniel 8 and 9. All we know about it is that after this season of tribulation, there will be a great divine judgment and God's kingdom will rule in fullness. "A time, times and half a time" refers to however long a period stretches between the inauguration of God's kingdom and the final judgment.

So far, this vision has added the idea that the progression of nations will be like a succession of beasts, and that God's kingdom expansion will end with a general divine judgment. Important stuff. But for the most important detail, Daniel had to look up.

A Son of man

> As I looked, thrones were set in place, and the Ancient of Days took his seat. His clothing was as white as snow; the hair of his head was white like wool. His throne was flaming with fire, and its wheels were all ablaze. A river of fire was flowing, coming out from before him. Thousands upon thousands attended him; ten thousand times ten thousand stood before him. The court was seated, and the books were opened …
>
> In my vision at night I looked, and there before me was one like a son of man, coming with the clouds of heaven. He approached the Ancient of Days and was led into his presence. He was given authority, glory and sovereign power; all peoples, nations and men of every language worshiped him. His dominion is an everlasting dominion that will not pass away, and his kingdom is one that will never be destroyed. (Daniel 7:9-10, 13-14)

Christians universally read this text from a New Testament perspective. We know Jesus and it is easy to find him represented here. But imagine receiving this vision before the New Testament. It shapes how the New Testament will be understood. It is clearly a vision of God, the Ancient of Days presiding over his court, utterly glorious and sovereign. Into his presence comes someone who remains distinct from God, and yet is treated fully as God in terms of his authority, power and right to our worship. The Old Testament is clear that there is only one God. Yet Daniel sees two persons treated like God.

"One like a son of man"—what an unusual phrase. A son of man means simply a man, a son of Adam, as it were. But how can a person be like God, and also be like a man? Daniel could not understand it. He simply saw it. He saw the one who, as a human being, will bring God's rule to earth for all nations and forever. It was a vision rather than physical reality, to be sure, and the figure may have been obscured by clouds. But Daniel saw him.

In the gospels, two related phrases are used of Jesus: "Son of God" and "Son of man." "Son of God" conveys the notion of a family relationship with God. Hence, those reconciled to God by Christ are also called "sons of God." "Son of man" is different. Out of context, the phrase could refer to anyone. But in the New Testament, it is a phrase forever connected with this vision of Daniel, and it refers to only *one* person. It refers to divinity in human form. It was Jesus' favorite way of referring to himself.

Looking into the New Testament

These visions are fundamental to biblical faith. Daniel did not have the New Testament to teach him these things or help him understand them. From our perspective, however, we see that this vision introduces God's people to the one who will later take the name, "Jesus."

The importance of Daniel's faith becomes increasingly clear. In the midst of losing everything, he chose to believe in God's sovereignty, that the tragedy he was part of was God's doing. Yet at the same time, he chose to believe in God's promise that he loves his people with an everlasting love. Daniel pinned his entire life on that larger faith. He was determined to believe, but he also wanted to understand, understand God's plan for the world and how Israel's exile and Israel itself was part of it. In response to Daniel's faith, God revealed his plan to him, a plan anchored in (future) real-world history that will use Israel to prepare the way for a divine/human being who, three empires later, would come to earth and begin the international expansion of God's kingdom.

This is not a New Testament teaching given after Christ. It is what Daniel saw in the sixth century BC. And hold on to your hat, because the visions keep coming.

For the Time of the End

Context: Daniel 8:1-27

"Gabriel, make this man understand the vision" …
So he came near where I stood. And when he came, I was
frightened and fell on my face. But he touched me and
made me stand up. He said, "Behold, I will make known to
you what shall be at the latter end of the indignation, for it
refers to the appointed time of the end." (Daniel 8:16-19)

Each of Daniel's visions revealed more of God's plan.
In yearning to know God's purpose for Israel's exile,
Daniel stumbled into something much larger than he
anticipated, because God's purpose for Israel will involve
every nation and establish the future of mankind. From
the first vision of the huge statue, Daniel saw that the
kingdom of God that was experienced and displayed in
Israel would explode upon the entire world in the midst
of a future empire three times removed from Babylon.
Daniel saw the rebellious nations of this world portrayed
as sub-human, bestial, and how our full humanity would
be restored in a kingdom ruled by a unique "Son of
man," a divine/human person who will both embody
and build God's kingdom on the earth.

In Daniel 8 we get more details of future history (future, from Daniel's perspective). And as a bonus, we are given three concepts that give us a vocabulary with which to speak of the period of kingdom growth from the appearance of the Son of man until the final judgment. A period known in the Bible as "the last days."

Magnifying part of the timeline

In this vision, Daniel sees himself in a personally familiar setting, in the provincial capital of Susa, along a recognizable canal. His vision highlights the first two empires that will follow Babylon. At this point, we are not surprised that they are represented by beasts, one a ram and the other a goat. We know that these beasts represent successive empires and for the first time, they are actually named. "The two-horned ram that you saw represents the kings of Media and Persia. The shaggy goat is the king of Greece" (vv. 20-21). Both of these kingdoms would have been known to Daniel.

Daniel first sees a two-horned ram (perhaps a ram was chosen because the zodiac symbol for Persia was Aries, the Ram). Media/Persia's expansion is represented by the ram irresistibly expanding to the north, south and west (from present day Iran). But then a goat (Greece) appears with a single prominent horn, which we are told represents the first king of Greece, which has to be the famous conqueror later known as Alexander the Great. The goat moves so fast that his feet don't touch the ground (the speed of Alexander's conquests was truly astonishing). The goat-kingdom expands from the west, overcoming the ram.

At the height of the goat's power, the horn is broken (Alexander will die at the height of his conquests). In its place rise four horns reaching out to the four winds (in all directions). Alexander's huge kingdom was divided into four parts, each ruled initially by one of his generals: Asia Minor, Macedonia and Greece, Egypt and Palestine, and Mesopotamia and Persia.

At this point, we must remember that, while this vision involves world affairs, its central point of interest is Israel. The vision, therefore, focuses on a small but powerful horn growing off of one of the four horns. It grew "in power to the south and to the east and toward the Beautiful Land" (vs. 9). This identifies the Seleucid segment of Alexander's divided empire, Mesopotamia and Persia, which expanded east to envelop the homeland of Israel. From this point on, the vision is about this little horn, who is the ruler of the Seleucid empire most associated with his impact on Israel. His name is infamous, Antiochus IV.

This is a great example of the nature of visions, especially "apocalyptic" visions concerning the last days. The last or latter days refer to what happens when the purpose of Old Testament national Israel is fulfilled, and God's kingdom breaks out into the world at large.[1] This has been the focus of all the visions of Daniel, tracing the succession of kingdoms between his day and the day when the Son of man crashes into the fourth beast-kingdom to grow the kingdom of God into a mountain covering the whole earth. The growth of the mountain defines the last days, the times when the purpose of Israel's calling is fulfilled in Christ. Apocalyptic visions were visions of that future. Because their content had not yet happened, they were not like photographs. Rather,

---

[1] Consider Isaiah 2:2, Micah 4:1-2, Hebrews 1:1-2, and Acts 2:17 (from Joel).

the prophet sees evocative pictures that express the *meaning* of what will happen, with sufficient detail to identify fulfillment when the subjects of the vision later come to pass.

Models of the future

This vision puts a magnifying glass on the second and third kingdoms of Daniel's vision: Media/Persia and Greece. It does not include the fourth kingdom (Rome), when the Son of man would arrive, yet Daniel is told that "the vision concerns the time of the end" (vs. 17). How can that be? How can it concern the time of the end, if it doesn't look far enough into the future to see the end's beginning with the coming of the Son of man?

Note that the interpreting angel goes on to say, "I am going to tell you what will happen later in the time of wrath, because the vision *concerns* the appointed time of the end" (vs. 19, emphasis added). The literal history of the little horn who will exalt itself to heaven is very important for understanding the *nature* of the last days which will come later in "the time of the end," when the sort of tribulation caused by Antiochus will be repeated over and over toward the church as it spreads the gospel across the world.

We find such models of the future all over the Old Testament, when an historical event or institution is designed by God to characterize Christ's later fulfilling work. Think of how the exodus from Egypt prefigures Christ's deliverance from sin, or how the priesthood and sacrifices explain Christ's cross. Historical models were more than models; they were important historical events and developments in their own right. But the New Testament can look back on them as models that illustrate the Person and Work of Christ (1 Corinthians 10:11).

That is what is happening now in this vision concerning Antiochus. The history of Antiochus' impact on Israel was all too real, some of the most difficult years in Israel's long history. Daniel is given a specific vision of this time period in order to give him (and us) a picture of what the entire era of the end times will be like. There is enough information for the Jews to identify the little horn when he later appears in person. But what we learn about him will be used by the New Testament to describe at least three concepts which are crucial to understanding the time of the end, which is the time in which we now live.

Antiochus IV

After Greece overthrew Persia and split into four parts, The "little horn" from the east would exalt himself greatly. The text mentions "the host of heaven" and "the Prince of the host," implying that events on earth reflect a parallel heavenly conflict, and we will hear more of this later in Daniel. The little horn is described thus:

> a king of bold face, one who understands riddles, shall arise. His power shall be great—but not by his own power; and he shall cause fearful destruction and shall succeed in what he does, and destroy mighty men and the people who are the saints. By his cunning he shall make deceit prosper under his hand, and in his own mind he shall become great. Without warning he shall destroy many. And he shall even rise up against the Prince of princes, and he shall be broken—but by no human hand. (Daniel 8:23-25)

A man of bold face (the word suggests insolence), deceitful, incredibly dangerous, thinking himself superior to everyone and everything, destroyer of God's people, willing to stand against God, himself. His predicted meteoric rise and unexpected demise reminds us that God has never lost control. Indeed, God makes use of him to prepare us for the last days.

Antiochus IV only exercised power for about 12 years, but in that time he successfully waged war in Egypt, Parthia and Palestine. His greatest atrocity is depicted in Daniels' vision of the little horn:

> It became great, even as great as the Prince of the host. And the regular burnt offering was taken away from him, and the place of his sanctuary was overthrown. And a host will be given over to it together with the regular burnt offering because of transgression, and it will throw truth to the ground, and it will act and prosper. Then I heard a holy one speaking, and another holy one said to the one who spoke, "For how long is the vision concerning the regular burnt offering, the transgression that makes desolate, and the giving over of the sanctuary and host to be trampled underfoot?" And he said to me, "For 2,300 evenings and mornings. Then the sanctuary shall be restored to its rightful state." (Daniel 8:11-14)

Antiochus IV "Epiphanes" associated himself with divinity (Epiphanes means "God manifest"). He appropriated the Jerusalem Temple for his own use. He ended the morning and evening sacrifices Moses established at God's command, removed the holy furniture designed to express God's holy grace, and placed a statue of Zeus on the Temple altar. There he offered profane sacrifices, including a pig, thus thoroughly defiling and desecrating the Temple. No greater offense could have been conceived by the Israelite mind. Israel had been called out of slavery to worship the Living God whose name lived among them in his Tabernacle and then Temple. That was their purpose. And for 2,300 evenings and mornings, that did not happen.

These 2,300 evening and morning sacrifices spanned 1,150 horrible days. Since Antiochus actually stopped the sacrifices a few months before he set up his own, this works out to be about three and a half years. It is said that having this prophecy of three and a half years of blasphemy later gave Israel hope when it actually occurred, for it promised that the sacrilege would not go on forever.

But the New Testament finds more in Antiochus. It finds three crucial concepts that give us the vocabulary, the colors and textures, to understand the times of the Son of man and the growth of his kingdom in this rebellious world.

Model 1: the abomination of desolation

The first is a phrase that does not appear here, but is based upon the content of this vision. Three times later in Daniel we find the phrase, "abominations that make desolate" (Daniel 9:27; 11:31; 12:11). All those references are linked to the discontinuation of sacrifices for three and a half years, so it is certain that they refer to the action of the "little horn," or Antiochus. The abomination that makes desolate, or, as the New Testament will phrase it, the abomination of desolation, is the defilement and misuse of God's Temple. The historical model was Antiochus, who wanted to end Israel as a theocratic nation.

The end times fulfillment was the defilement that led to the destruction of the Jerusalem Temple in 70 AD (Matthew 24:15; Mark 13:14), which actually did bring a permanent end to Israel as a national theocracy,[2] and henceforth identify God's kingdom as believers from *every* nation. Thus, Antiochus provides a descriptive marker Jesus used to declare that the last days had come, when the Son of man will take the gospel from Jerusalem and Judea and Samaria to the ends of the earth.

Model 2: the three and half years

Secondly, the little horn gave us a way to describe the indefinite time period of gospel expansion. Historically, the Temple would be shutdown by Antiochus for three and a half literal years. Daniel first heard this time reference describing the persecution that would begin with the fourth beast and end with final judgment (Daniel 7:25-27). He will hear it again (Daniel 9:27) when it describes the period between Christ's first and second coming. Daniel heard it once more (Daniel 12:7) describing the period when God gathers a multitude to everlasting life.

As we will see in a careful study of Daniel 9, this reference is used to symbolically describe an intentionally indefinite period (not even Christ knew the precise timing of his return). If we need to reference an indefinite time period of tribulation under Rome and the rubble of nations that Rome spawned, the three and a half years of Antiochus' rule is a meaningful candidate.

In the Book of Revelation, this designation of three and a half years of tribulation is mentioned three times.

---

[2] A modern nation of Israel was formed in 1948, but this is a secular state, not a theocratic one acknowledging the Lord as King by following his Law.

There, it is not meant to be literal, and it is not meant to be confusing. The Apostle John's vision simply used the term as Daniel did. Israel's historic experience under Antiochus conveniently describes the indefinite period of: 1) the ongoing witness of the church (Revelation 11:1-3), 2) the ongoing persecution of the church (Revelation 12:6,14), and 3) the ongoing rebellion of the nations (Revelation 13:5) throughout the period of gospel expansion.

Rather than describe the last days as "an unknown length of time," it is called some version of three and half years. The memory of Antiochus reminds us that it will be a time of ongoing tribulation, and also that it is limited and will have an end.

Model 3: antiChrists

Third and finally, Antiochus, the little horn, becomes the historical reference for anyone who attempts to take God's place in his own Temple. Antiochus did not actually claim to be God Almighty; he erected a statue of Zeus in the Temple. Antiochus claimed to be God's manifestation, the one who represented and interpreted God in this world. According to Antiochus, God was much better understood by a statue of Zeus than the Ark of the Covenant. Antiochus was, therefore, anti-Yahweh, anti-the God of Israel—"anti" not so much in the sense of being against as being instead of.

The New Testament picked up on this idea by speaking of "anti-Christ." The word antiChrist is used four times in the New Testament, not of a single person but of anyone who takes Christ's place in God's Temple, that is, in his church. The Apostle John said that "antiChrist" described a spirit already evidenced in his own day (1 John 4:3). Both times that Jesus spoke of the abomination of desolation, he talked about false Christs (plural). Paul specifically warned his elders that church leaders would later arise who would try to lead disciples after themselves (Acts 20:28-31). False apostles and teachers are mentioned the New Testament, and the spirit of antiChrist is featured in the Book of Revelation as a second, *religious* beast who supports the worship of the principle beast, or state (Revelation 13:11-12).

Antiochus is the historical model of all antiChrists who try to replace the biblical Christ *in his own church*. They falsely claim to represent the Living God, i.e., to be Christian, but in reality turn the worship of the Lord into a fabricated idolatry. Paul described the work of antiChrists perfectly …

> I am afraid that as the serpent deceived Eve by his cunning, your thoughts will be led astray from a sincere and pure devotion to Christ. For if someone comes and proclaims another Jesus than the one we proclaimed, or if you receive a different spirit from the one you received, or if you accept a different gospel from the one you accepted, you put up with it readily enough. (2 Corinthians 11:3-4)

The abomination of desolation that inaugurates the troubled era of gospel expansion, the symbolic three and a half years that promise this period of tribulation is limited and one day will end, and the antiChrists who put themselves forward among God's people so as to obscure the Lord, himself … all these images come from Daniel's vision in Daniel 8. They show how central Daniel was to the New Testament understanding of the gospel era.

Make Your Face to Shine

Context: Daniel 9:1-23

"And now, O Lord our God, who brought your people out of the land of Egypt with a mighty hand, and have made a name for yourself, as at this day, we have sinned, we have done wickedly.

"O Lord, according to all your righteous acts, let your anger and your wrath turn away from your city Jerusalem, your holy hill, because for our sins, and for the iniquities of our fathers, Jerusalem and your people have become a byword among all who are around us. Now therefore, O our God, listen to the prayer of your servant and to his pleas for mercy, and for your own sake, O Lord, make your face to shine upon your sanctuary, which is desolate. O my God, incline your ear and hear. Open your eyes and see our desolations, and the city that is called by your name. For we do not present our pleas before you because of our righteousness, but because of your great mercy. O Lord, hear; O Lord, forgive. O Lord, pay attention and act. Delay not, for your own sake, O my God, because your city and your people are called by your name." (Daniel 9:15-19)

Not every Jewish captive's faith remained intact after Babylon shredded their personal hopes, humbled their nation, sacked their capital, laid waste to their Temple and kidnapped their brightest and best. Many would fear

God's abandonment or his defeat by the gods of Babylon. To survive required a larger faith, as illustrated by the refugee named Daniel. He chose to believe in God's total sovereignty, that the things that happened did not occur in spite of God, but because of God. Babylon was victorious because God decided that his own rebellious people would benefit from being separated for a time from their inheritance. They would illustrate the Lord's reaction to sin, and then later his grace in forgiveness. Daniel chose to submit and devote his life to God's sovereign purpose, whatever that would mean for him.

Anselm of Canterbury famously affirmed, "I do not seek to understand in order that I may believe, but I believe in order to understand." In a way, that was Daniel's experience, not because faith automatically gave him insight, but because God rewarded his faith with a revelation of his purpose. As to no one ever before, God revealed to Daniel details of his purpose for Israel in his ultimate plan to redeem the world. Daniel was first shown a timeline of future empires marking a ballpark time reference for the arrival of God's kingdom on earth. Then Daniel received a magnified look at a brief, future period of woe, a time of tribulation for God's people under a man later known as Antiochus IV Epiphanes. That vision tattooed into Israel's awareness images that would later interpret the longer period of tribulation accompanying the worldwide spread of God's kingdom. And most amazingly, Daniel saw a bright sign in the night sky revealing a Son of man who would personally bring God's kingdom to earth. Daniel kept giving himself to God's purpose and God in return kept revealing his purpose as he had to no one previously.

If Daniel's visions had ended with Daniel 8, he would be hailed as one of the greatest and most blessed prophets of all time. But Daniel's faith was not exhausted, and neither was God's response.

Godly prayer

Daniel was carried into Babylon in 605 BC in fulfillment of Jeremiah's prophecy of a 70 year exile. The language of Daniel 9:1 is a bit obscure, but it clearly references the first year of the succeeding Persian Empire, which in our reckoning was 539 BC. While 70 years had not yet passed, Daniel hoped that with the change of administration, the Lord might consider the purpose of the exile completed. He therefore took to heart God's promise through Jeremiah,

> For thus says the Lord: When seventy years are completed for Babylon, I will visit you, and I will fulfill to you my promise and bring you back to this place. For I know the plans I have for you, declares the Lord, plans for welfare and not for evil, to give you a future and a hope. Then you will call upon me and come and pray to me, and I will hear you. You will seek me and find me, when you seek me with all your heart. I will be found by you, declares the Lord. (Jeremiah 29:10-14)

Daniel's larger faith believed God's Word that, regardless of the foreign superpowers involved, he would bring Israel back. He also believed God's Word that the Lord would do so in response to being sought afresh. Daniel therefore devoted himself to seeking God with all his heart, in the hope that God would respond by bringing to pass what he had promised. Thus, Daniel demonstrated two fundamental principles of biblical prayer.

The goal of prayer is to seek God

Many needs move us to pray. Just look at a typical prayer list and you will see health, success, the welfare of loved ones, security—all the things people typically want. Thank God that we have the good sense to respond to our sense of need by praying. But prayer is not fundamentally about listing our desires. Faith turns our desire into a search for God, a search to know him, to know all things through him, to trust him, to live and walk with him. Faith understands that God is our Creator who understands us better than we understand ourselves. Faith understands that God is our Redeemer, and intends our good in every situation. Therefore, faith understands that God alone can fulfill our desires, and God alone knows which desires to bless. Faith in the Lord believes that his will for us is always better than our will for ourselves.

God decreed a painful exile that turned his people temporarily into refugees, so that they would find in him their eternal home. God said that when the lesson was learned, he would bring them back to their inheritance. And how would they get there? By seeking him with all their heart. God created us with the unique ability to have personal relationships because God desires to have relationships with us. God is not lonely or needy. God simply wants to express his inner being, revealing it through the space and time he created, with creatures able to know him and share his love.

Do not be anxious, saying, "What shall we eat?" or "What shall we drink?" or "What shall we wear?" For the Gentiles seek after all these things, and your heavenly Father knows that you need them all. But seek first the kingdom of God and his righteousness, and all these things will be added to you. (Matthew 6:31-33)

We are free to speak to the Lord of our needs, although he learns nothing from the exchange. He already knows what we need. And he also knows that what we need *most* is to know him and find joy in his righteousness, joy in his kingdom and his purposes.

Daniel listened to what Jeremiah had said, and understood this. God knew their needs and fully intended to bring them back to their homeland. But only when they sought him with all their heart, and not before. Because more important than where they lived was that they would live in him. More important than our health, or security, or the welfare of our loved ones, is that we know the Lord and live in him. In our anxiety, we may not always believe that. But God always does.

And so did Daniel. This, too, was part of his larger faith. The desire to see Israel return motivated Daniel to seek answers. But his faith in God's Word through Jeremiah understood that he needed to seek God more than any answer. So Daniel focused on relationship.

O Lord, the great and awesome God, who keeps covenant and steadfast love with those who love him and keep his commandments, we have sinned and done wrong and acted wickedly and rebelled, turning aside from your commandments and rules. We have not listened to your servants the prophets, who spoke in your name to our kings, our princes, and our fathers, and to all the people of the land. (Daniel 9:4-6)

In the ancient world, "personal relationship" was expressed by the idea of "keeping a covenant." Covenants were committed relationships with both explicit and implicit expectations. The examples that readily come to mind are marriage and government treaties. But any committed relationship was a covenant, be it legal, informal or implied. Even a firm friendship had the sense of a covenant (cf. 1 Samuel 18:3), because each friend knew how they could count on the other. In God's covenant with Israel, God committed himself to unearned, forgiving favor from his heart, and God's people committed themselves to obedient trust from their heart. This reflected the relationship God created humanity to share with him. The point of redemption, which is the story of the Bible, is to restore with many the relationship God originally intended—in the poetry of prayer, to see his smile again (making his face to shine).

Everyone in exile wanted to stop living as refugees and go back home. But Daniel's larger faith focused on the relationship, or covenant, between God and Israel that needed to be restored. More important than just getting home was learning to trust God again, and trust is experienced as obedience. Daniel's prayer, therefore, concentrates on confession. Israel was in the state it was in because they refused to listen to God's prophets and turned away from God's commands. Daniel cites the repeated warnings from God which went unheeded, warnings made to both Israel's leaders and citizens.

As always, the problem had not been simply ignoring some rules. Daniel confessed to God that Israel was scattered because of "our unfaithfulness to you." Unfaithfulness is a personal thing. Adultery is wicked, not because it violates a rule, but because in violating a rule, it violates a relationship. That's what "covenant" is all about: what two committed parties may expect of each other. God does not cherish his rules. He cherishes his people and desires for us to cherish him. That requires trust that God deserves first place, and that God has our best interests at heart.

Restoring a strained, distant or broken relationship with God always involves confession. It always involves our confession of sin because the Lord has never wandered from his love and commitment; we are the unfaithful ones. In the absence of Israel's kings and priests, Daniel takes on the role of a mediator. He confesses sin on behalf of the whole nation. He takes on the nations' sins as his own. He confesses how "we" have sinned and how God's judgments have rightfully fallen on "us." He asks for God's forgiveness and fresh favor, a restoration of the covenant relationship God had made with Israel so that they would see his face shine upon them again.

The focus of prayer is God's character and promises

It is important to remember that the kind of relationship we need with God is not defined by us. A child is not a good choice to define parental love. An abusive husband is a poor choice to define marital bliss. Daniel bases his plea for a restored relationship on God's character—the divine name which God's own actions have exalted. The Lord will always be faithful to us because he is always faithful to himself. His integrity is absolute. Asking God to do something foreign to his character never works, while depending on his character never disappoints.

Daniel is confident in God's forgiveness because of who God is. "We do not make requests of you because we are righteous, but because of your great mercy" (vs. 18). Just as our sin is a manifestation of our broken character, God's faithfulness is a manifestation of his perfect character. If we are in covenant with him, we do not need to wonder about God's grace, forgiveness and love; we may assume it and rejoice in it. That leaves us free to concentrate on our trust and obedience so that we may again experience a whole and healthy relationship with the Lord.

God's perfection implies that when it comes to asking for specific things or a specific favor, prayer should focus on God's promises. Divine promises are not loopholes believers can leverage to force God's hand. Promises highlight God's motives in creation. The purpose of the universe is to reveal God's personal and invisible nature in the interactions of space and time, and especially through his interaction with people. If God simply wanted to do this or that, or have that or this happen, he would simply do it. His plans would unfold automatically. But that is not why God made humanity. Mankind exists to accomplish God's will as a "family business" that teaches us even as we interact with him.

That is why the most important of God's plans and actions are structured around promises and prayer. Jeremiah said that when the benefits of the exile were complete, God would bring his people home—not automatically, but in answer to prayer. God calls his people to seek him with all their heart and ask him to fulfill his promises, so that when he answers they may know with all their heart that they have found *him*. We learn who God is as he accomplishes his declared plans in answer to our prayers.

The essence of sin is to create our own gods (idols) and try to get them to make the world what we want it to be. It is a strange and foolish way to look at reality: sometimes comically, sometimes tragically, but always a pathetic attempt to tattoo small bits of meaning on the universe.

Daniel had a larger faith. He believed that the meaning of all things, all of life and history, including his life and history, rested in the Living Creator God. We find this Living God when we believe what he has historically revealed about his plans, and then see him bring his declared will to pass in answer to our prayers. Daniel prayed, asking God to forgive and honor his initial covenant with Israel, bringing them home in a new exodus. And God did what he promised to do, what he wanted to do—in answer to Daniel's prayer.

It is of the essence of faith to believe not only that God's will is preeminent, but that God's will for us is always better than our will for ourselves. The best strategy for prayer was uttered by David upon learning of God's extraordinary plans to bless him,

And now, O Lord God, confirm forever the word that you have spoken concerning your servant and concerning his house, and *do as you have spoken*. And your name will be magnified forever. (2 Samuel 7:25-26, emphasis added)

Do as you have spoken; do what you have promised. David could think of no greater thing to ask for. Jesus said it most simply: "Father … your will be done."

Daniel surely desired for Israel to return home, but he asked God to do it because that is what God had promised. The covenant love of God is not a reality because we want it (our desires are so unstable anyway). The covenant love of God is eternally and unchangeably ours for the embracing because God wants it. We know that because of the redemptive promises God has made, accomplished ultimately in Christ, and now fulfills in response to our prayers.

More than he asked for

The Book of Daniel is not only about the larger faith of its author. It's also about how God responds to such faith. This prayer illustrates how God's intended purpose for the exile was fulfilled in Daniel and any others like him. He had sought the Lord—sought to know the Lord for who he truly is, and trusted that the best thing God could do for his people would be to fulfill his promises.

So pleased was the Lord in Daniel's faith that he would now proceed in a vision to place the promised return from exile into the much larger framework of *all* his redemptive promises. Daniel longed to see the purpose of Israel's exile fulfilled so that his people might return home. The Lord responded to Daniel by revealing to him the fulfillment, not only of Israel's exile, but of Israel's entire redemptive purpose—the coming of the Son of man, his work of redemption, and the last days of this age when God's kingdom grows into a mountain that fills the earth. And the Lord would reveal all this to Daniel in greater detail than to anyone else in the Old Testament.

Seventy Weeks

Context: Daniel 9:24-27

"Seventy weeks are decreed about your people and your holy city, to finish the transgression, to put an end to sin, and to atone for iniquity, to bring in everlasting righteousness, to seal both vision and prophet, and to anoint a most holy place. Know therefore and understand that from the going out of the word to restore and build Jerusalem to the coming of an anointed one, a prince, there shall be seven weeks. Then for sixty-two weeks it shall be built again with squares and moat, but in a troubled time. And after the sixty-two weeks, an anointed one shall be cut off and shall have nothing. And the people of the prince who is to come shall destroy the city and the sanctuary. Its end shall come with a flood, and to the end there shall be war. Desolations are decreed. And he shall make a strong covenant with many for one week, and for half of the week he shall put an end to sacrifice and offering. And on the wing of abominations shall come one who makes desolate, until the decreed end is poured out on the desolator." (Daniel 9:24-27)

There can be no greater testimony to Daniel's larger faith than Gabriel's observation that God Almighty "greatly loved" him (vs. 23). It is because of God's appreciation of Daniel's faith that he gives a vision of the future such as no one had yet received.

Daniel 9 has been interpreted in several different ways, depending to some extent on the presuppositions brought to this amazing text. I respect other points of view, and I certainly claim no infallibility. What follows is my understanding, consistent with my take on the rest of Daniel, and also the Book of Revelation. To me, Daniel and Revelation are bookends.

The reader will be excused for being tempted to skip this chapter. It is tedious because it requires a number of careful distinctions. This vision of the future is both uncommonly specific and necessarily vague. Specific leaders are mentioned, but not named. Specific time frames are mentioned, but in unusual ways. Specific deeds are mentioned, but no details about how they are accomplished.

This is because, of all visions, this one especially had to accomplish two goals. First, it was designed to predict the future with jaw-dropping accuracy and clarity, so that the culmination of ancient Israel's purpose could be unmistakably associated with Jesus Christ. But second, it also had to be sufficiently obscure *until the things predicted came to be*. As with earlier predictions concerning the exile and second exodus, Daniel's prophecy needed to be sealed, filed away, so it could be interpreted properly *after* the events took place (compare Isaiah 8:16 with Daniel 12:4). Why? Because prophecies vindicate God's purpose in things to come; they do not cause them to happen.

This had been true of Jeremiah's prophecies, and Isaiah's earlier prophecies regarding the exile. They did not bring about repentance and avoid the exile, neither did they cause the exile. But because Isaiah predicted future events in remarkable detail, faithful ones like Daniel could later see, after the fact, that the exile was part of God's plan. The prophecy of Daniel 9 was not given to cause Christ to come, but rather to authenticate the later work of Christ and explain the nature of the last days.

Such prophecies require us to fill in intentionally obscure details that only become obvious with later history. We come to this prophecy desiring to understand it as Daniel would have, yet we cannot help but understand it better, because we live after its fulfillment. This does not mean that the prophecy means whatever we want it to mean. It has a very specific structure. When the details are later filled in, the prophecy snaps together perfectly.

That being said, there are many pieces to snap together and sometimes it feels like you could use a third hand. But it will be worth the effort when it is done. Here we go …

The Jubilee of Jubilees

The prophecy of Daniel 9 is structured by a time reference harkening back to Leviticus 25:8 which reads, "Count off seven sabbaths of years — seven times seven years — so that the seven sabbaths of years amount to a period of forty-nine years." Seven sevens of years were used to calculate the next Jubilee year, celebrating God's redemption and Israel's inheritance with the forgiveness of debt. Because of how the week is structured as seven days in Genesis, seven was a number of special importance in the Old Testament, suggesting completeness. Thus, rather than say that the Jubilee is every fifty years, they said it comes after seven sevens of years. With that ancient model in mind, consider Daniel's prophecy:

> Seventy weeks are decreed about your people and your holy city, to finish the transgression, to put an end to sin, and to atone for iniquity, to bring in everlasting righteousness, to seal both vision and prophet, and to anoint a most holy place. (Daniel 9:24)

If seven sevens announced a standard Jubilee, then seventy sevens announced a final, super Jubilee of God's redemption, the final forgiveness of all debts and the arrival of our eternal inheritance. Opportunity to transgress God's law will be finished, sin will end, and wickedness will be atoned for. God's righteousness will become the norm on earth forever, visions and prophecies will all be fulfilled, and all that is holy will be consecrated. This indicates the full completion of God's redemptive plan, including the work of Christ, the expansion of God's kingdom, Christ's return, the judgment of God and the inauguration of the new heavens and earth. On the analogy of the standard Jubilee year, seventy sevens describes a time frame of 490 years for all this to happen. This period is subdivided into several sections.

> Know therefore and understand that from the going out of the word to restore and build Jerusalem to the coming of an anointed one, a prince, there shall be seven weeks. Then for sixty-two weeks it shall be built again with squares and moat, but in a troubled time. (Daniel 9:25)

Although Daniel knew that Cyrus ordered a rebuilding of the Temple, we know that the decree to restore and rebuild Jerusalem would not come until later, with Governor Nehemiah in 445 BC. That marks the beginning of the seventy-sevens of years. The first seven sevens, or 49 years, is a standard Julibee-like period in which Jerusalem is rebuilt. The following sixty-two sevens are a "troubled time" of great suffering for the Jewish people, characterized by the short but horrendous reign of Antiochus IV. After that, that is, after a total of sixty-nine sevens (483 years), another ruler, or prince shall come. This one would actually bear the name "anointed one," Messiah in the Hebrew, and in the Greek, Christ.

> And after the sixty-two weeks, an anointed one shall be cut off and shall have nothing. (Daniel 9:26)

Seven sevens plus sixty-two sevens of years after Nehemiah (483 years), someone would arrive to accomplish the purposes mentioned earlier: to atone for wickedness and bring in righteousness. It is not hard for Christians to guess who this refers to, especially since "cut off" is the language used in "cutting (making) a covenant." The covenant made with Abraham was "notarized" by the cutting of animals, in that instance representing the substitutionary death of God himself (Genesis 15, compare vs. 6 with Romans 4:3 and Galatians 3:6). Daniel is told that 483 years after the future decree to restore Jerusalem, the anointed one (the Christ) will come, and soon thereafter would become the covenant sacrifice Abraham saw in his vision, a death which would atone for wickedness and establish God's righteousness in us.

Could this possibly be accurate? Many think that all the calculations of Daniel 9 are symbolic. But it is not difficult to check them out. 483 years after 445 BC brings us to … 37 AD. This is disappointing, because it does not correspond to Jesus. Jesus was anointed as Messiah at his baptism in 30 AD, and was crucified over three years later in 33 AD. Daniel's prophecy seems to overshoot this.

I will never forget the day I was studying Babylonian culture and noted in passing that, like ancient Israel, they used a lunar calendar. The above calculations assume a modern *solar* calendar. Solar calendars have 365 days per year, so 483 years would be 176,295 days. Lunar calendars have only 360 days per year, so 483 years would be 173,880 days, which is 2,415 days *less*. This puts the end of the sixty-ninth year and the anointing of Christ's ministry at … 30 AD. Six centuries before Christ, Daniel was told exactly when the Son of man would come, and what he would do.

Before moving on with this prophecy, let's consider the enormity of what we've already found. This is an astounding prediction of Jesus Christ. Not even the most critical scholar believes that Daniel was written after Jesus. Pinpointing the year of his anointing from centuries before did not make Jesus happen, but it powerfully vindicates that he is the one who brings the kingdom of God to earth. The implications are so staggering that it raises necessary questions about whether this is a reasonable interpretation.

The true meaning of Christmas

But there is striking biblical evidence that this is not a novel interpretation. This evidence has been hidden in plain sight since the formation of the New Testament, and is celebrated by all Christians every Christmas. Everything about the narrative of Christ's birth is saturated in Hebrew tradition except one anomaly which, while dearly loved, makes little apparent sense. The Wise Men. Why were Persian Magi involved at Christ's Nativity? How did they get there? The common belief is that they saw a new star which for some reason they thought announced the birth of a king, and they followed it every night until it led them to Jerusalem, and finally to Bethlehem. But a plain reading of Matthew 2 shows that this is not what happened.

The Wise men did not follow a star to Jerusalem. They saw a sign in the sky ("star" could have been anything), but they did not follow this star to Jerusalem. It was only after their confusing interview with Herod that they *again* saw the sign which they had seen before in the east, and this time, they followed it the last five miles to Bethlehem (Matthew 2:2,9-10). OK, but if they didn't follow a star from Persia, how did the Wise Men know to visit Jerusalem?

There is endless speculation about what the "star" might have been, a supernova, a conjunction of stars or astrological construct, but no such heavenly display could lead them the five miles from Jerusalem to a specific location in Bethlehem. Add to this, the fact that no one else saw this "star," not ancient astrologers or anyone in Israel. The Wise Men were the only ones to follow it to Bethlehem because they were the only ones who could see it (if anyone could see it, Herod would have followed it himself).

The only explanation is that what they saw in Persia, and then again in Israel, was a bright *vision* in the heavens meant for only them to see—very much like Daniel's bright vision in the night sky of the Son of man. And this at once explains how they knew to go to Jerusalem. Centuries after Daniel, there were still a few who treasured the writings of history's greatest Magi. They were looking for a Son of man who would bring God's kingdom to earth for all nations during the fourth empire, the Roman one. But when? Daniel told them it would be 483 years after a decree which, for them, was a matter of historical record (Nehemiah). They expected the Son of man to be recognized in what we call 30 AD. If they saw a vision like Daniel's three or four decades before this date, they would reasonably assume that it heralded the Son of man's birth.

The Wise Men did not follow anything to Jerusalem. They went to Jerusalem because Daniel's prophecy told them who they would find (the Christ), where they would find him (Israel), and that he had just been born (given that his work would occur in his adulthood). When Herod proved clueless, they rejoiced in *again* seeing the vision, low enough in the sky for them to follow to a very special place in Bethlehem.

This interpretation of the sixty-nine sevens is the only biblical explanation that accounts for the Wise Men. Their unexpected arrival ties Old Testament prediction to New Testament fulfillment. Every Christmas, these Wise Men remind us that the divine Son of man brought a kingdom for *all mankind*. Therefore these Gentiles came, they bowed down, and they worshiped. They came because of

Daniel's larger faith, anticipating the Great Commission even at Christ's birth.

The Last Days

> And the people of the prince who is to come shall destroy the city and the sanctuary. Its end shall come with a flood, and to the end there shall be war. Desolations are decreed. And he shall make a strong covenant with many for one week, and for half of the week he shall put an end to sacrifice and offering. And on the wing of abominations shall come one who makes desolate, until the decreed end is poured out on the desolator. (Daniel 9:26-27)

The last week (seven years) of this prophecy follows the work of the Son of man to its finish, launching into the difficult last days with a promise that no matter long they may be, they will come to an end. The final seven years is divided in the middle, which is to say into two halves of three and half years. At the close of the first half, there will be an end to sacrifice and offering. From our perspective, this parallels what Gabriel said earlier about finishing transgression, putting an end to sin, atoning for wickedness, and bringing in everlasting righteousness. That is, it speaks of the end of the Old Testament sacrificial system, when Jesus presented himself as the atoning sacrifice which the animal sacrifices had portrayed (Hebrews 9:11-14; 10:11-14). Christ's death on the cross atoned for the sin of God's people once for all, making them forever righteous in God's sight. Jesus was crucified in 33 AD, about three and half years after he was first identified as the Anointed One, the Christ, at his baptism. The veil of the Jerusalem Temple was torn in two, the way to God was opened, and the symbolic purpose of the Temple fulfilled. This ended the need for sacrifices and offerings (Hebrews 9:24-26).

Looking back at this prophecy after Jesus' work makes it easy to see the correlations. The timeline Daniel first received as a statue of four segments had now become a detailed calendar stretching across 486½ years to pinpoint Christ's death on the cross. Truly amazing.

But what of the last half of the seventieth week? According to Gabriel, the end of the seventieth week marks the complete fulfillment of God's redemptive plan, when all vision and prophecy is fulfilled and a new holy place is sanctified for God's people. The end of Daniel's vision also sees the final judgment outpoured. In other words, the end of the seventieth week is the end of the age, the end of the last days, when Christ returns to judge the world and consecrate a new heavens and new earth.

All in three and half years? Was all this supposed to happen by 37 AD? Clearly not. What is going on? One popular modern theology arising out of the British Zionist movement of the mid-1800s speculates that there is an unmentioned "gap" in Daniel's prophecy at this point, when the prophetic clock is "stopped," to restart again three and half literal years before Christ's return. However, while such a gap must be theorized in order to justify the view of modern Israel championed by Dispensationalism, there is no biblical ground for it.

And such theorizing is completely unnecessary. We have already seen how the literal three and half years under Antiochus' abominable desolation became a symbol of tribulation throughout the last days. That is not a convenient bit of theological slight of hand. That is exactly how the reference is used in Daniel 7:25 where it is "a time, times and half a time." There, it describes the period (identified with the Roman Empire and the tumble of modern nations descended from it) when the saints of the Most High are persecuted. This is the same period when God's kingdom expands like a mountain over all the earth. We are told there that at the end of this period, the Son of man will bring judgment, and all the kingdoms of this world will become the kingdom of the Most High (Daniel 7:26-27). Apparently, "three and half years" uses the historical literal oppression under Antiochus IV to symbolically represent the entire period of tribulation from Christ's cross to his return. Daniel has already used the reference in exactly this way.

The Book of Revelation understands this time reference as part of the vocabulary given by Daniel to describe the whole gospel era. Revelation 13:5 directly parallels Daniel 7, referring to the era when the beast oppresses the people of God (and in Revelation, the beast is an amalgam of all of Daniel's beasts). In that instance, it is phrased as "forty-two months" which, of course, is three and half years. The period is also mentioned twice in Revelation 12, once as 1,260 days (exactly three and half years according to a lunar calendar), and once as "a time, times and half a time." Both of these periods refer to the opposition of Satan against both Jewish and Gentile believers, beginning with Christ's ascension and continuing until his return.

While all the other time references in Daniel 9 are precise, the last three and half years is not. It is a symbol, used multiple times, taken from a season of great tribulation in Israel's history. Such a symbol is necessary because the last days from Christ's resurrection to his second coming *has to be indeterminate*. The time of Christ's return will not be known until it happens. Not even Jesus in his humanity knew that date. What better code for tribulation under a succession of beasts and antichrists than a number recalling the literal tribulation under Antiochus, who was associated with one of the original beasts and was the model of all antiChrists? As with Antiochus, it is a promise that no matter how long the tribulation goes, it *will* come to an end. Not to mention, it perfectly rounds out the seventy week prophecy.

We are living now in the "three and a half years" of tribulation under Satan's opposition, experienced under a succession of beast-like states and antiChrists determined to lead the church away from its Lord. It is a difficult time as Satan furiously battles the expansion of God's kingdom. But the gates of hell simply cannot stand against it.

The Destruction of Jerusalem in 70 AD

> And after the sixty-two weeks, an anointed one shall be cut off and shall have nothing. And the people of the prince who is to come shall destroy the city and the sanctuary. Its end shall come with a flood, and to the end there shall be war. Desolations are decreed.
>
> And he shall make a strong covenant with many for one week, and for half of the week he shall put an end to sacrifice and offering. And on the wing of abominations shall come one who makes desolate, until the decreed end is poured out on the desolator." (Daniel 9:26-27)

The last issue to clarify is the identity of figures who appear during the final week, described as "an anointed one" (vs. 26), "the prince who is to come" (vs. 26), and "one who makes desolate" (vs. 27). We should note that one verse earlier (vs. 25), the terms "anointed one" and "prince" are linked to describe one person who is "coming" (in that case, Nehemiah). Unless there is a compelling reason not to, we should see the two references in vs. 26 as also linked to the same person, an anointed one whose coming rule is positively anticipated. "One who makes desolate" (vs. 27), refers to a completely different person.

"An anointed one shall be cut off and shall have nothing" (vs. 26). As we have already noted, this refers to the arrival of Jesus, the Son of man, at the beginning of the seventieth week, anointed by his baptism in 30 AD. The prophecy declares that he will be "cut off" sometime after the seventieth week begins. That happened three and half years later on the cross.

"And the people of the prince who is to come shall destroy the city and the sanctuary. Its end shall come with a flood, and to the end there shall be war. Desolations are decreed" (vs. 26). No specific time reference is given; the destruction is simply linked with the anointed prince. Jerusalem was smashed and its Temple destroyed in 70 AD by the Romans. But this interpretation would link the Romans who destroyed the Temple to Jesus Christ. How come?

Remember the initial premise behind Daniel's faith at the beginning of his journey. Nebuchadnezzar destroyed Jerusalem and its Temple, but was unwittingly a tool in the hand of the Lord. Similarly, Roman Commander Titus destroyed Jerusalem and its Temple, but was unwittingly a tool in the hand of Jesus. Jesus proclaimed to the Sanhedrin leaders that, to their dismay, he would be revealed as Daniel's Son of man who would come in power and glory (Mark 14:62). Jesus declared that the national leaders' rejection of him would result within one generation in the destruction of the Temple (Matthew 24:1-2ff, explained by Matthew 23:29-39, cf. vs. 34). The destruction of Jerusalem and the Temple in 70 AD by the Romans thus unintentionally vindicated Jesus' identity as the sovereign Son of man (Matthew 24:30).

The Roman legions did not follow the Lord Jesus any more than Babylon worshiped the Living God. But when the legions brought down the institutions that had rejected Christ, they were carrying out what God had decreed and Jesus had prophesied.

The New Covenant

"And he shall make a strong covenant with many for one week" (vs. 27). The great hope of the Messiah, especially as preached in Daniel's boyhood by Jeremiah, was the formation of a new covenant, a "strong" one which succeeded where the law and sacrifices had proven weak, strong to penetrate hard hearts with God's redemption. Jesus proclaimed this covenant immediately from his baptism on, proclaiming that God's kingdom had arrived in him. After Christ's ascension, the apostles began the worldwide spread of this good news. Every Christian, whether Jew or Gentile, has become part of this new covenant. Thus, he made a strong covenant with many for the entire seventieth week, which began with Jesus' preaching and continues throughout the gospel age.

For the three and half years that Jesus preached, the old and new covenants overlapped. But after his cross and resurrection, "for half of the week he shall put an end to sacrifice and offering," because the old covenant had been laid aside. The way into God's presence which the old Temple and sacrifices could only picture, Jesus achieved in reality. The old sacrifices and old religion had served their purpose and were no longer needed during the last three and half years that symbolically make up the gospel age.

"And on the wing of abominations shall come one who makes desolate, until the decreed end is poured out on the desolator" (vs. 27). Jesus tied this verse in Daniel to the destruction of Jerusalem and the Temple (Mark 13:14-20). This could refer to the Roman desecration of the Temple in 70 AD. Or, it could refer to the way Jewish leadership assured the Temple's destruction through their perversion of Old Testament teachings. The later option should be considered, since Jesus accused Jewish leadership of displacing God with their own traditions (Mark 7:6-8). He actually declared that the Jewish leadership had desecrated the Temple's function (Luke 19:41-46). That's what Antiochus did.

There are a great many prophecies of Christ in the Old Testament, from major themes to specific details. But none is more remarkable than this prophecy that pinpoints Christ's arrival and his work, and sketches the major characteristics of the era of gospel expansion. God gave such an extraordinary vision to Daniel because he held the man in high esteem. Since we know that it is faith that pleases God, we assume that it was Daniel's larger faith that led to a larger vision of God's plan, one that spans all of human history.

A Great Conflict

Context: Daniel 10:1-21

> In the third year of Cyrus king of Persia a word was revealed to Daniel, who was named Belteshazzar. And the word was true, and it was a great conflict. (Daniel 10:1)

The last of Daniel's recorded visions takes up most of Daniel 11 and 12. It concerns "a great war," the battles and legacy of misery left by Antiochus IV Epiphanes, which for Daniel still lay in the future. Daniel 10 is simply an introduction to this vision, recording the meeting of Daniel and a heavenly messenger. But for just a moment and almost by accident, as if looking beyond the angel through a heavenly door he came through before it closed, Daniel sees another vision. Behind the wars of Antiochus, indeed, behind all the machinations of every world power and every earthly conflict, Daniel sees a corresponding conflict in heaven. This was not the message that the angel came to give, but it was a revelation powerful enough to overcome the prophet, and worthy of our consideration all on its own.

An unexpected messenger

Two years after King Darius allowed the various peoples uprooted by Nebuchadnezzar to return to their ancestral homes, Daniel spent three weeks in mourning, something so important to Daniel that his fasting overshadowed and displaced his Passover observance.

We are not told why Daniel was so distressed. He must have rejoiced when the Jewish aliens were allowed to return home. Perhaps he was mourning for fear that those returning were not prepared to learn from their experience. Perhaps it was for reasons similar to Nehemiah years later—that Israel's cities, culture and Temple were still in ruins. Since those who returned were more than a generation removed from knowing Israel first hand, they would arrive as aliens in their own land. The suffering had not stopped, and was likely to continue a long, long time.

> On the twenty-fourth day of the first month, as I was standing on the bank of the great river (that is, the Tigris) I lifted up my eyes and looked, and behold, a man clothed in linen, with a belt of fine gold from Uphaz around his waist. His body was like beryl, his face like the appearance of lightning, his eyes like flaming torches, his arms and legs like the gleam of burnished bronze, and the sound of his words like the sound of a multitude. And I, Daniel, alone saw the vision, for the men who were with me did not see the vision, but a great trembling fell upon them, and they fled to hide themselves. (Daniel 10:4-7)

In earlier visions, the messenger bringing visions was called Gabriel, an angel. This time, no name is given. The angel Michael is mentioned later, but this figure is not identified. One cannot help but note similarities between this description and the one given by the Apostle John when the risen Jesus spoke to him (Revelation 1:10-15), right down to John's collapse before receiving a strengthening word and touch. One also thinks of Paul's encounter with the risen Christ on the Road to Damascus (Acts 9:3-7), when others heard Jesus' voice but did not see him. Those were manifestations of the risen Jesus, but they were also visions (Jesus does not literally have a sword coming out of his mouth). The point is that the vision Daniel saw is very similar to visions of Christ, and a *vision* of the pre-incarnate Son is just as possible as a *vision* of him resurrected.

However, the text clearly says that this figure was sent by God (vs. 11), a phrase which usually refers to an angel, and indeed, it may be that this is the same Gabriel who was sent twice before. On the other hand, the Father also "sent" his Son. It is impossible to be certain who this is, only that he is personally engaged in a heavenly battle on our behalf (vs. 21). Actually, it is because this messenger was hindered so long in battle that I doubt he is the Son of God. In my judgment, Daniel received a vision of an angel, I will assume Gabriel, and the vision of Christ given John in Revelation was intentionally made similar in order to intentionally tie together those men and their visions.

If I may be allowed a small rhetorical flourish from my old preaching days, I will observe that while most of us would do well to fall to our knees in humility before a messenger from God, Daniel's humility was such that he had to be *raised* to his knees after having already fallen prostrate (vv. 9-10). Daniel is again praised, this time as "a man greatly loved" by God (vs. 11).

Then he said to me, "Fear not, Daniel, for from the first day that you set your heart to understand and humbled yourself before your God, your words have been heard, and I have come because of your words. The prince of the kingdom of Persia withstood me twenty-one days, but Michael, one of the chief princes, came to help me, for I was left there with the kings of Persia, and came to make you understand what is to happen to your people in the latter days. For the vision is for days yet to come." (Daniel 10:12-14)

This is the vision within a vision Daniel received, a glimpse of a heavenly conflict connected to the earthly conflicts Daniel saw. Gabriel explains why he was "late" in responding to Daniel's prayer for understanding. He says that he was dispatched by God to answer Daniel's prayer on the first day Daniel prayed. That was three weeks earlier. For all that time, he had been hindered by "the prince of the kingdom of Persia," and only arrived after of the intervention of Michael, a "chief prince."

Michael was the name associated with an archangel. The fact that he is called a chief prince implies that the "prince of the kingdom of Persia" also refers to an angel. So, with a polite explanation of why he is late, Gabriel opens the door a crack to reveal a massive conflict in heaven involving opposing angels. And the conflict in heaven is somehow linked to what we experience.

The rest of Daniel 10 describes Daniel's physical weakness after his fast, and the accommodation of his heavenly visitor to aid him. The vision of glory seems to be replaced with one of a simple human being. While it is possible that this was a different visitor, it is also possible that the visionary form of Gabriel's presence was adapted to something less overpowering. Thus, a warm and reassuring human touch raised the elderly Daniel to his feet with assurances that he was loved.

Gabriel then tells Daniel that before he must return to engage the princes of Persia and Greece, he will reveal a portion of what he calls "the book of truth," which, as we will see, records a future conflict involving remnants of the Greek Empire. This earthly conflict will have a devastating effect on Israel, but through Daniel, God reveals that an end to the misery will be coming, and that God has everything under control.

Before we move on to look at this last extended vision given to Daniel, let's consider for a moment this vision-within-a-vision of heavenly conflict.

Spiritual warfare is real

Jesus taught us to pray regularly for deliverance from evil—literally, "the evil," and therefore possibly, "the Evil One," the devil (Matthew 6:13). The Bible is unequivocally clear that the devil is real, a personal angelic being who chose to rebel against God. At the same time, there is frustratingly little detail about his motives and goals.

The most insightful information comes from two Old Testament texts about ancient kings, one of Babylon and one of Tyre (Isaiah 14:3-15; Ezekiel 28:1-10). Each text compares a human king with a heavenly being. It is likely that they are being compared to the devil. If so, these texts indirectly give us a sketch of this angelic person, who is called "the morning star" in Isaiah 14:12. The morning star is Venus, and the Latin name for Venus is Lucifer. As this being struggles against God and his people, he is also called Satan, from a Hebrew word for "adversary."

The scathing verbal attacks against two corrupt kings suggest that that Satan was the greatest of God's angels, one who was tasked to look after the magnificent planet, Earth. Much to the angel's surprise, however, God entrusted dominion of this world not to him, but to creatures molded in God's image out of the planet's dust. Ever since, Satan has endeavored to demonstrate the error of God's choice. At every opportunity, the devil works to dehumanize the human race, turning "the image of God" into a broken and immoral mockery of the Creator. But rather than stopping him, the Lord has seen fit to allow him limited freedom for the duration of this age, using his own malice against him (for example, letting Satan arrange for the cross, which was his downfall).

The Apostle John received a vision of the same heavenly conflict Daniel heard about. John saw the devil as a dragon.

> Now war arose in heaven, Michael and his angels fighting against the dragon. And the dragon and his angels fought back, but he was defeated, and there was no longer any place for them in heaven. And the great dragon was thrown down, that ancient serpent, who is called the devil and Satan, the deceiver of the whole world—he was thrown down to the earth, and his angels were thrown down with him. (Revelation 12:7-9)

Lucifer and a number of angels who rebelled with him (often called demons) are now malevolently involved with humanity. In the gospels, we see demons dehumanizing people mentally, physically and morally. Satan personally focused on Jesus. Having only made matters worse by engineering Jesus' death, Lucifer and his followers now spitefully focus more of their strength on breaking down those who follow Christ (Revelation 12:13-17).

Superstition is real, too

The problem is that every culture has customs, stories, myths and beliefs about a devil. While the enlightened brush him off, multitudes construct elaborate superstitions about how to deal with him. Both approaches only serve to keep the real Lucifer hidden. As C. S. Lewis said,

> There are two equal and opposite errors into which our race can fall about the devils. One is to disbelieve in their existence. The other is to believe, and to feel an excessive and unhealthy interest in them. They themselves are equally pleased by both errors, and hail a materialist and a magician with the same delight. (from the Preface of *The Screwtape Letters*)

There has arisen in the church an almost magical approach to spiritual warfare that tries to influence the course of the heavenly conflict by using specific prayers, rituals and incantations. Satan is happy to see us distracted by such superstition, because it is completely ineffective. Not even using "the name of Jesus" as an incantation will dominate the devil (Acts 19:11-17). God's Word actually forbids us from pronouncing judgment upon Satan (Jude vv. 8-9), although that will change upon Christ's return (1 Corinthians 6:1-3). We are not in Satan's league, and we aren't supposed to be.

In Daniel 10, we catch a glimpse of spiritual warfare as it is experienced in heaven. Daniel is also involved in spiritual warfare, but not by trying to fight it in heaven.

Daniel does not pray about what the angels are doing. He mourns over Israel's failure and asks for forgiveness and grace. He does not ask God to do anything with Satan; he does not refer to Lucifer or address him in any way. He is praying to understand Israel's future (vs. 12), how God's glory and his people's good can be consistent with their weakness and misery. His fasting and prayers are not a ritual to summon spiritual power. Rather, they express profound weakness, confusion and mourning. Daniel is not trying to control the future or tell Gabriel (or God) how to do his job. He falls down before God to seek his face, confess his sins, and ask the Lord to fulfill his promises.

In this regard, consider the Apostle Paul's most famous statement about spiritual warfare, Ephesians 6:10-20. He tells us that we battle against spiritual (angelic) powers. But he does not recommend superstition, like saying prayers with special words of power or doing special rituals. Paul instructs us that our part in spiritual warfare involves grasping the truth, living righteously, sharing the gospel, using our faith to deal with trials, making our salvation sure, studying and believing the word of God, and praying all the time for the needs of God's people and guidance for those who proclaim the gospel. None of this involves anything magical or ritualistic. None of it is an attempt to personally get direct power over Satan. We daily pray for deliverance from Satan, but we don't need to personally overpower him. All we have to do is follow Jesus in our obedience, and as he causes the gates of Hell to fall, we just walk behind him right over the Evil One (Matthew 16:17-18; Romans 16:19-20).

If Daniel 10 gives any specific insight regarding spiritual warfare, it's to ask God's mercy upon our government and the governments of other countries. It is highly unnerving that rebellious angels should be called the "princes" of associated nations. It reminds me that Jesus called Satan "the ruler of this world" (John 12:31; 14:30; 16:11), and the Apostle Paul called him "the prince of the power of the air" leading "the course of this world" (Ephesians 2:2). It suggests that Satan invests much of his effort to dehumanize nations through leaders of government and cultural institutions.

There is no question that the Lord answers the prayers of his people offered in faith and with a desire to see his will accomplished. God accomplishes his will largely in response to our prayers. The point here is that "spiritual warfare" does not describe a different or enhanced kind of prayer or ministry in the heavenly realms. Heavenly warfare is a different dimension of the same war we are in every day, a dimension we are not directly a part of even though we are in the same fight. God does link our prayers with what he is doing both in heaven and on earth, but we do not run the show and tell the angels their strategy. We simply exercise obedient faith in whatever patch of this world we touch, knowing that when God graciously decides to accomplish his will in concert with our efforts and prayers, he commands a heavenly host capable of moving anything in heaven and on earth to make it so.

The War Room

Given what they had seen in World War I, Britain's military expected up to 200,000 casualties from bombing in the first week of the next war. Realizing that the populace would feel abandoned if the Prime Minister and the government fled London, they determined to create an emergency shelter. Hence, a secret "War Room" was constructed in a reinforced basement of offices in Whitehall. Churchill's War Cabinet met there 115 times. Here were the strategic maps, markers and intelligence that guided decisions about Dunkirk, the Battle of Britain, and other engagements.

On the streets and in the homes of London, people contributed to the war effort as best they could. Some sent sons and husbands into the military. Some filled extra roles to keep society going. Some tended small gardens and watched other people's children. Everyone did something right in front of them, according to their gifts and opportunity. And truly, everyone had a hand in their ultimate victory.

Imagine, however, a young boy delivering a sandwich to someone in Whitehall, taking a wrong turn, and then another, inadvertently passing by the War Room just as someone was coming out. For one, maybe two, tantalizing seconds, he would have seen ... not the big picture, but people who saw the big picture. Models of Spitfires engaging German bombers, naval operations to hunt U Boats, and who knows what else. He would leave knowing that there *was* a big picture, and he could go home confident that the chaos around him was not incomprehensible to the people directing things, and he was part of it all as he delivered meals to Whitehall!

Spiritual warfare is like that. God does not expect us to take on angels who incite mayhem in the United States or Iran or North Korea. Instead, every Christian has something to do right in front of him or her, according to each one's gifts and opportunity. As we walk with God's

Holy Spirit, as we pursue righteousness, obey the Word, share the gospel, and pray normal, biblical prayers for God's will, we will all truly have a hand in the ultimate victory.

But because an angel was late on his assignment, we glimpse a conflict fought and managed at another level. Daniel was not invited through that door, and neither are we. But while we may struggle to understand the chaos around us, we know that there *is* a big picture, and we can each do our bit with confidence because the Lord of Hosts knows what he is doing.

That is exactly what Daniel needed to know as he drew near to the last vision he will receive, a whirlwind of data about tribulation that would be overwhelming, except for the fact that it was all revealed ahead of time, and therefore, must be part of that bigger picture controlled by the Living God.

Like the Stars

Context: Daniel 11:1-12:4

> And those who are wise shall shine like the brightness of
> the sky above; and those who turn many to righteousness,
> like the stars forever and ever. (Daniel 12:3)

Daniel 11 and 12 record the earthly conflict linked to
Gabriel's battles in heaven (Daniel 10:12-14) when he
teamed up with the angel Michael (Daniel 12:1). Please
read the entire context, as I will give just an overview. For
us, what is described here is now history (between 100
and 300 BC), but for Daniel, it concerned the future. As
previously, there is significant detail, but without names,
places, specific dates and explanations. Such a vision
could not cause the future to happen, but looking back, it
would convincingly authenticate that this was, indeed, a
vision of the future, and therefore, under God's control.

This vision outlines the forces that would cause Israel
tribulation for the next few hundred years after Daniel. It
speaks of the Persian Empire and its fall to Greece, of
rulers that include Xerxes and Alexander the Great. Of
special interest is the future terror under Antiochus IV
Epiphanes, who desecrated the Jewish Temple and
declared himself the manifestation of God on earth.

20-20 hindsight

Daniel 11 is indecipherable to most people, but a treasure trove to history buffs of that period. We have a myriad of details of ongoing conflict between the "North" and "South," the North being the Seleucid branch of Alexander's Empire centered in old Babylon, and the South being the Ptolemaic branch centered in old Egypt. Every detail can, in retrospect, be convincingly attached to real figures, real places and real battles. Let me give just a single verse as an example:

> His sons shall wage war and assemble a multitude of great forces, which shall keep coming and overflow and pass through, and again shall carry the war as far as his fortress. (Daniel 11:10)

"His sons" are the sons of Seleucus II, Seleucus III (reigning from 226-223 BC) and Antiochus III (223-187 BC). "Shall wage war" refers to the battles led by these two against Ptolemy III. "As far as his fortress" means that the Seleucids penetrated to Ptolemy's fortress in southern Palestine at Raphia. Most of this section can be filled in with such historic details, including marriage alliances, betrayals and military reversals.

How do we know all this? The same way a Civil War buff can explain to you in detail the movements of Robert E. Lee's Army of Northern Virginia or Sherman's march through Georgia once you give him a few general geographic references and points on a time line. Those places and times would have no special meaning before the Civil War, but became memorialized afterwards.

What is most important is to realize that this back and forth of war is happening where these ancient superpowers came together geographically, in Palestine and the land of Israel. The horrific bloodshed experienced there really had nothing to do with Israel directly, but nonetheless afflicted generations of Jews. Think of Israel as a soggy WWI style trench in no man's land, repeatedly changing hands in the blood-soaked conflicts of foreigners who are always on their way to somewhere else. And while this is going on, the Temple is desecrated for partisan purposes and must be rededicated.

Verses 14-15 chronicle some choices made by Israelite factions, but it soon becomes clear that Israel cannot even control which side will oppress them. We see here the development of a Jewish identity as a ravaged people, people whose home, culture and religion are repeatedly raped by outsiders. The ultimate indignity is recalled again in verses 21-39, with the reign of terror under Antiochus IV, whose three and half years of defilement inspired the later concepts of an abomination of desolation and antiChrist.

Tribulation

Why so much detail about the troubles and tribulations of this period? Because it gives us an historical model of the end times, the gospel age of Jesus Christ.

A connection with the end times ("the time of the end" of Daniel 11:40) is characterized from two perspectives. First, Daniel 11:40-45 describes battles which never happened during the Seleucid/Ptolemaic wars—stylized battles which sound like the ones mentioned earlier but have no specific historical reference and seem to stretch from the first century BC to the final judgment (Daniel 12:1-2).

Then that *same* period of tribulation is described as a consequence of spiritual warfare under Archangel Michael's watch (Daniel 12:1-2). The point seems to be that while the horrors of Antiochus will be literal and tragic, they also set the tone for God's people during the rest of history, as we take part in the spiritual conflict that expands the kingdom of God.

This means that the tribulation of God's people does not refer to a short season at the tail end of the gospel age, but the gospel age *itself*. During the gospel age following Christ's death and resurrection, Christians will experience hardship much like that experienced by Israel under Antiochus. From an earthly perspective, Christians will be trampled in unending wars and worldly conflicts which we cannot control. Sometimes these conflicts will even be aided by corrupt churches which need to be rededicated to Christ. In every century and every decade, Christians will be run over as nations continually grab power from each other, stepping over peacemakers as they go from one place to another.

From a heavenly perspective, that same tribulation is the aftershock of spiritual warfare that is growing the stone into a mountain. Bringing the gospel to a warring world is not easy.

But regardless of the motives of the nations in their constant violent maneuverings, Christ is always extending his kingdom into every one of them. It is hard, it is painful and costly to expand Christ's church while the world is in constant war with itself, but that is exactly what Jesus is doing through us. Christians must concentrate on building Christ's church through a myriad of social crises which cannot be ignored, and in fact are the very places in which gospel faith will take root. Let me say that more pointedly. It is the upheaval of tribulation that prepares the soil for gospel seeding.

And sometimes, we must do all this with one hand tied behind us, because part of the church has decided to worship something other than the biblical Lord Jesus, canceling our gospel witness just where and when it is most needed. When that happens, then in addition to reaching the unbelieving world, we must also rededicate Christ's Temple (us). Whew!

Will it be worth the effort? In a word, "Yes!"

At that time your people shall be delivered, everyone whose name shall be found written in the book. And many of those who sleep in the dust of the earth shall awake, some to everlasting life, and some to shame and everlasting contempt. (Daniel 12:1-2)

The book of life, the death of the body as temporary sleep, the resurrection of all mankind, final judgment leading to everlasting life or shame ... It's all here, first revealed so plainly to Daniel, who in his youth devoted himself to a larger faith.

With the end of this section, Daniel's recorded visions come to a close, and he will have done for succeeding generations, what Isaiah and Jeremiah had done for him. As before under Nebuchadnezzar, so again under Antiochus Epiphanes, General Titus of Rome, and a host of tyrants since, it will often appear to God's people like he has utterly abandoned them. In spite of all their efforts to follow Christ, worldly abominations seem to have the last word ... *except* ... except the prophets of the Living God have convincingly declared all this beforehand. That means that even our tribulation is part of God's sovereign plan, and is linked to the heavenly campaign that will complete his eternal kingdom.

Daniel's prophecies would give Jews the larger faith they needed to persevere under Antiochus until the Temple could be rededicated, a faith which they still commemorate during Hanukkah, the Festival of Lights. And these same prophecies can give Christians a larger faith today to persevere on the earthly side of spiritual warfare. A faith that brings the gospel and Spirit of Jesus to everyone who needs him, confident that the brokenness and pain of this world are not out of God's control. In fact, our tribulation actually paves the way for the gospel. And, praise God, even the greatest difficulties shall come to an end in due course.

Those who have the larger faith to believe this are the ones who will turn many to righteousness and shine like the stars forever.

Go Your Way

Context: Daniel 12:5-13

> Then I, Daniel, looked, and behold, two others stood, one on this bank of the stream and one on that bank of the stream. And someone said to the man clothed in linen, who was above the waters of the stream, "How long shall it be till the end of these wonders?" And I heard the man clothed in linen, who was above the waters of the stream; he raised his right hand and his left hand toward heaven and swore by him who lives forever that it would be for a time, times, and half a time, and that when the shattering of the power of the holy people comes to an end all these things would be finished. I heard, but I did not understand. Then I said, "O my lord, what shall be the outcome of these things?" He said, "Go your way, Daniel, for the words are shut up and sealed until the time of the end. (Daniel 12:5-9)

In dramatic fashion, Daniel's final vision comes to the now aged Magi by way of three heavenly figures. They are not named. One might assume that the two figures on either side of river are angels, perhaps Gabriel and Michael, for they have appeared earlier. The figure over the water is more enigmatic. The fact that he swore by God that the visions were true would seem to indicate that he, too, is an angel. But God swore by his own name to Abraham (Genesis 15:17-21; cf. Hebrews 6:13-18), so it is possible that this figure in some way represents the Lord in this vision, perhaps the Christ-like figure of Chapter 10 who appeared in glory before transforming into one of the sons of men. We can't be certain.

It is this last figure who announces the full time frame of Daniel's visions. The prophet already knew that his visions describe a time long after his life on earth. He had been told that the Son of man's work of redemption was still over 500 years away. And the last vision of Chapters 11-12 ended with vague references to an indeterminate time of tribulation stretching all the way to a future resurrection and judgment of all who had ever lived. It is this last-referenced indefinite time period which the figure over the water describes as "a time, times, and half a time." And this symbol is mentioned yet again in vs. 11, using Antiochus' desecration of the Temple to describe the entire period from the end of Jewish sacrifices to the resurrection of the dead, i.e., from Christ's first to his second coming.

Daniel's response: "I heard, but I did not understand. Then I said, 'O my lord, what shall be the outcome of these things?'" From our perspective, we can see, name and date everything up to Christ's first coming. Daniel saw the structure, but lacked the historical detail we have. He was overwhelmed and wanted to know yet more.

Daniel was told that the level of detail he wanted would be sealed and available to no one until all was fulfilled. Daniel's prophecy was not about shaping the future. Rather, it was Daniel's privilege to one day vindicate God's sovereign plan once the Son of man came. Perhaps one of the details he would have appreciated knowing was the meaning of the two dates mentioned in vv. 11-12 that tweak the standard three and half years reference. I'd like to understand that, myself.

Live with a larger faith

The last command to Daniel was to "Go your way" (vs. 9). Go your way? Daniel had been given the perspective of a soaring eagle over the next several empires, close-ups of Israel's greatest tribulation, and an epic view of the last days with eternal life on the horizon. No one before had ever seen these things. Beside Jesus, no one would see these things again except the Apostle John, who connected Daniel's visions to the last days, which John would witness at their beginning. Daniel has seen the plan of Almighty God for the redemption of the world, and now he is simply told to "Go your way"?

How strange to modern ears, especially American ones. Surely, Daniel is supposed to do something with all this information. Sell books (he did write one, but did not sell it), make a movie, do a series of Ted Talks, advertise the "secrets of the future" on YouTube. Surely, Daniel could leverage this information to influence the king and change society.

No. "But go your way till the end. And you shall rest and shall stand in your allotted place at the end of the days" (vs. 13). See your life in the perspective of all God is doing through time, and use that insight to fuel what God has called every believer to do, which is to live a life of faith and faithfulness, no matter what. You have done that, beloved Daniel. So go your way, go to sleep, and at the proper time, rise forever to receive the inheritance reserved for you.

At the end of Daniel's Babylonian journey, he attained in full what he devoted himself to at the beginning, a larger faith. Marching across the desert as a captive teen, Daniel humbly decided that the evil and pain he suffered was happening not in spite of God's good will, but because of it. On the strength of that faith, Daniel chose to exchange all his hopes and dreams for whatever God had for him, regardless of what that was. For the rest of his life, Daniel did not seek wealth or power or fame (though he received all those things). Whether serving in his career, or using his spiritual gifts, or sharing his faith, or living his faith, Daniel sought the Living God.

What he found was that through many trials, the Lord is taking the world someplace amazing, and walking with him on the journey is ultimately all that matters.

Discussion

Into Nebuchadnezzar's Hand

Read Daniel 1:1-4

1. Make a list of things (physical, mental, emotional, social, spiritual) that Daniel lost when he was taken to Babylon.

2. What was Nebuchadnezzar's purpose in taking Daniel?

3. This chapter mentioned two men who may have served as heroes to young Daniel. Who were they, and why were they special?

4. Why do you think Daniel believed that the Lord God was still in control? Do you think you would feel that way?

The King's Food

Read Daniel 1:5-21

1. What do you think of the argument in this chapter about why Daniel arranged to eat simply?

2. Describe some situations in which it would be hard to say "No" to someone because they control something important to you.

3. How important is fellowship in keeping God first? How important are private spiritual disciplines?

4. Name some contemporary influences that cause many Christians to drift from living like Jesus.

5. Give some examples of how Christians might work together to keep God in first place today.

A God Who Reveals Mysteries

Read Daniel 2:1-30

1. Why do you think the Lord gave Nebuchadnezzar the dream, instead of just giving it to Daniel?

2. How do you understand the relationship between faith and science?

3. Daniel's record of God's revelation became part of the Bible. Do you think of the Bible as God's revelation to you? What does that mean?

The Stone That Became a Mountain

Read Daniel 2:31-49

1. How did the great statue in the dream function as a timeline? How much information did it provide? What information was not yet revealed?

2. Do you think God knows the future? What does that say about God's control?

3. If God has a kingdom of his own, what does that say about all other kingdoms?

4. Would you say that the universal victory of God's kingdom is a wish, or a future fact? How does your opinion make.a difference in your life? How could it make a difference?

But I See Four Men

Read Daniel 3:1-30

1. Explain the significance of Nebuchadnezzar's big event. Describe some contemporary situations that create pressure for Christians to conform.

2. How do you think Shadrach, Meshack and Abednego had the strength to remain faithful to God?

3. Can you give an example of a government-favored religion? What has that done for the government? for the religion?

4. What principles would you use to determine when to submit to an authority, and when not to?

The Most High

Read Daniel 4:1-37

1. What sorts of temptation naturally press upon people with power?

2. Given Daniel's advice, describe how God wants civil leaders to function, whether or not they believe in him.

3. In what sense do human societies function in a sub-human way? Give some examples.

4. Do you think Nebuchadnezzar felt that he had been cursed or blessed? Can you think of examples when being humbled has proven in some way beneficial?

Weighed in the Balances

Read Daniel 5:1-31

1. What does it mean today when someone "sees the handwriting on the wall?"

2. Why did Daniel tell Nebuchadnezzar's story before he interpreted the writing?

3. Share some things that parents tend to learn from painful experience, which they want their children to learn without going through the pain.

4. Do you think everyone must learn what Nebuchadnezzar learned, one way or another?

The Lion's Den

Read Daniel 6:1-28

1. How were Daniel's enemies motivated? How did they get the king to make such an outlandish law?

2. Describe some ways Daniel could have hidden his prayer life, and thus avoided arrest.

3. How did Daniel's experience parallel what his friends went through with the fiery furnace? What

does that tell us about the tension between civil power and religion?

4. Do you think you would be prepared to respond to such a threat as Daniel did? Why do you think he was prepared to do what he did?

5. What makes a faith like Daniel's potentially dangerous to leaders who crave power?

One Like a Son of Man

Read Daniel 7:1-28

1. Why do think God's visions repeatedly represent empires as beasts? What might be some appropriate animal candidates for our nation?

2. How is it significant that God's kingdom is not represented by a beast, but rather by a son of man?

3. With this vision in mind, which of the two phrases: "Son of God" and "Son of man" most implies diety? Explain why you think so.

4. If this passage were all that you had (i.e., no New Testament), what would you know about the one who rules God's kingdom?

For the Time of the End

Read Daniel 8:1-27

1. Do all biblical prophecies point to fulfillments which are still in our future, or have some already been fulfilled? Describe how we can identify the "little horn."

2. Why was it important for the Jews to have a prophecy about Antiochus before he appeared? What do you know the Jewish feast of Hanukkah? (Look it up if it would help.)

3. How does Antiochus define the concept of an abomination of desolation?

4. How does Antiochus give meaning to the time frame of three and half years?

5. How does Antiochus provide us with the model of what will later be called antiChrist?

Make Your Face to Shine

Read Daniel 9:1-23

1. What had to happen before the Lord would fulfill his promise to bring Israel back to their land?

2. Do you think Daniel was right to own Israel's past sin as his sin?

3. Discuss the goal of prayer. How does it relate to the many requests that we naturally make to God?

4. Discuss the focus of prayer. How important is it to pray according to God's character and promises?

Seventy Weeks

Read Daniel 9:24-27

1. The persons and actions portrayed in this vision could not have been recognized until they

occurred. What does that tell us of the purpose of such visions?

2. How do the explanations in Daniel 8 of the abomination of desolation and the three and a half years help us interpret Daniel 9?

3. Does the Wise Men's part in Christ's Nativity (Matthew 2:1-12) say anything about the accuracy of Daniel's vision?

4. Daniel just wanted to know about Israel's future concerning the 70 year exile. What did God decide to show him?

A Great Conflict

Read Daniel 10:1-21

1. What do we know about the spiritual warfare going on in heaven among angels? Who is the devil? What is he doing?

2. Discuss the quote from C. S. Lewis.

3. Daniel's prayer in Daniel 9 initiated maneuvers among angels. Did Daniel know that? Did he have to know?

4. What do you imagine are some of the big issues being dealt with in God's War Room right now?

5. Discuss how Daniel models what Paul says in Ephesians 6:10-20 about our part in spiritual warfare.

Like the Stars

Read Daniel 11:1-12:4

1. The period of the second and third centuries BC were miserable for Israel. How would Daniel 11 encourage them during that time?

2. Do you think history has born out the prophecy that not only Israel in the past, but also the church will undergo regular hardship and corruption?

3. "It is the upheaval of tribulation that prepares the soil for gospel seeding." Agree or disagree?

4. What does Daniel 12:1-2 say will happen at the end of all tribulation?

5. Spend some time discussing Daniel 12:3.

Go Your Way

Read Daniel 12:5-13

1. Daniel glorified the Lord in ways that we still talk about. Yet none of it was intentionally planned (by him). Why do you think the Lord chose to work through him so much?

2. Think about the difference it makes when you see yourself as part of something much bigger than your life and your lifetime.

   Would that make it easier to focus on what is important? (vs. 3)

   Would it make it easier to fall asleep in Christ? (vs. 13)

Notes

Personal Reflections

I've studied Daniel for years, even preached through it. But this book came during a time of transition: COVID-19, the upwelling of outrage over America's persistent racism, the multiple crises of the Trump administration, and my recent retirement after forty-four years of pastoral ministry. This has raised issues of personal identity, continued usefulness and mortality. I've come to Daniel to learn more about his faith. It's a strange book, in a unique biblical context, yet I have sensed the Author (and I don't mean Daniel) speaking to me.

And that is the point of studying Scripture, isn't it? To sense the Lord God speaking to you, not apart from the text, but through it.

This time through, I've been struck how different from mine is the mix of "active" and "passive" in Daniel's faith. I live in 21st century America where faith is something of an entrepreneurial activity. Faith always has to be "having an impact" on life and society. Exercising faith means taking the initiative in having an impact, working hard to make things happen, whether it is making the church grow or changing the way people think. All that makes sense to an American, and perhaps is a correct contextualization of Christian faith.

And yet, I see absolutely none of that in Daniel. I don't see Daniel taking a faith initiative in anything. The highest ranking administrator in an empire and chief of its scholar-priests, and I see no evidence of any campaign to change things—change policies or even change thinking patterns. Yet, clearly he did change thinking patterns, and may even have changed some policies under Nebuchadnezzar. Not to mention how he has inspired billions of people down the ages whom he never met. Daniel's faith was mostly passive on the outside, yet had a much greater impact than the faith initiatives I've been bred to appreciate.

At the same time, I can't miss the lengths Daniel was willing to go for no other reason than to be faithful to God—no expectation of reward, no attempt to "make a difference." Just simple faithfulness. I spent three years in seminary studying hard, debating, praying and practicing to prepare myself for service. But none of that was as personal and private and soul-shaping as three years of daily eating vegetables with friends in order to forge a committed and resilient character. Daniel never put himself forward to speak. When called to speak, however, he did not weigh consequences, but spoke the truth with candor. When obviously targeted for destruction, he again paid no heed to danger, but focussed only on faithfulness. Daniel's faith was extremely active on the inside, motivating faithfulness as the only thing that mattered.

It is apparent, therefore, that all of Daniel's remarkable success was due to being favored by God. He did not work for any of it. He worked hard, but he did not work for "success." And I don't just mean that he didn't work for money and prestige; he did not even work for God's blessing. Like his three friends, he knew that God could bless him, but never presumed that God would, even in a lion's den. Not even his desire for God's blessing mattered more to Daniel than being faithful to the Lord God Almighty.

It seems to me that Daniel gave up all his dreams for this life, trusting that God would give him whatever was best—best for God's kingdom and best for him, too. He did not even try to tell God what that was, but accepted each day, each situation and each opportunity from his hand. In response, the Lord made it abundantly clear that he appreciated and enjoyed this kind of faith.

This time going through Daniel, I looked for connections between his visions and his faith. It seems clear that Daniel received these visions because of his faith, and at the same time his faith was strengthened by the visions.

All Daniel's visions stood in stark contrast to his experience. A refugee and servant through no choice of his own, Daniel received the most impressive visions in the Old Testament concerning the scope of God's kingdom. There had been revelation before that God's kingdom would include Gentile nations, but Daniel saw actual empires and the shadows of actual historic figures. Daniel's own faith had to have been influenced by Jeremiah's prophecy of Babylonian victory as part of God's sovereign plan. In the same way, Daniel's predictions concerning Antiochus and Jesus Christ can have the same impact on my faith, especially as I face realities I do not enjoy and cannot control.

It is the specificity of Daniel's prophecies that make him quite the target of scholars, many of whom are uncomfortable with the whole idea of supernatural revelation. It is often taught that the large scale visions of Persia, Greece and Rome, along with the multitude of details in Daniel 8, prove that Daniel was written by others as late as the second century BC. That way, all the "future" parts were created after they had, in fact, already happened. And many insist that the seventy weeks prophecy involves abstract symbolism unrelated to actual history.

That's not what I found. The plain reading of Daniel 9 is a stunning prediction of the work of Jesus. As I mentioned earlier in the book, no scholar believes that Daniel was written *after* Christ. But that prophecy would still be convincingly supernatural if provided by someone in the second century BC, making the bias against Daniel's authorship pointless. In addition, for me, Daniel's authorship is compellingly underscored by the Wise Men of the Nativity. There is simply no biblical justification for a plain reading of the Matthew text except the application of Daniel 9.

I've come to see faith a little more as Daniel did, a vision of God's redemptive work that is much larger than my lifetime, and therefore much larger than my life. I find that I look at worldwide plague a little differently. I look at large social movements a little differently. I look at the actions of political leaders a little differently. The importance of those things, their tragedy or goodness, has not changed. But I feel much less that things might be out of control. Things may be out of my control, out of our control, and out of our leaders' control, but God is sovereign. The Lord knew all these things before they came to be, and if he knew them, then they represent the flow of history God intended to work with.

My responsibility to change things is much smaller than I realized, and my responsibility to be faithful no matter what is is much larger than I realized. Along with millions of others, God uses my faithful prayers and my faithful actions to accomplish his will. I am linked in Christ to a great conflict involving the heavenly host, a conflict which I cannot see, yet benefit from every day because I'm on the winning side.

Though I know more than Daniel (only by hindsight), like him, I still have questions. I still get weary. But I take heart that although the Lord Jesus asks everything from me, in the end, it's really quite simple. I have only to go my way being faithful, knowing that in due course I will arise to an eternal inheritance allotted to me by grace.

By Glenn Parkinson

Like the Stars - a Christian alternative to culture war

Should Christians be fighting a "culture war?" Seven key Bible insights outline how evangelicals can recapture their potential to enrich life in America.

Share Your Master's Joy - a partnership that lasts forever

Stewardship is finding joy in managing all of life to God's glory. Such joy pleases the Lord and directs his choice of future leaders.

Living Faith - convictions that bring faith to life

A faith to live by requires convictions rooted in God's Word. Here are fourteen powerful convictions, each illustrated by a character study from the Bible.

Tapestry - the Book of Revelation

The Book of Revelation was never meant to be a puzzle. The greatest challenge is not understanding it, but rather believing it shows us the real world as God sees it. When we see the world as God does, the most important thing in life becomes crystal clear.

A Larger Faith - the Book of Daniel

The Book of Daniel does more than simply demonstrate faith. By documenting a series of extraordinary predictive visions given to Daniel, it describes the worldview that naturally enlarges faith among God's people.

About the Author

Dr. Glenn Parkinson has been learning and preaching the Bible for over forty years. Converted while completing his undergraduate degree in physics, Glenn's goal is to discover the themes and patterns that weave God's Word into a coordinated and meaningful whole. And as a Reformed Pastor (Emeritus), he believes that every truth should be used as an engine for living in ways that please the Lord.

Glenn lives with his wife and best friend, Micki, and also a cat who constantly battles the keyboard for attention.